EMPOWERING WOMEN THROUGH PARTICIPATORY METHODS

EMPOWERING WOMEN THROUGH PARTICIPATORY METHODS

DR SHIVANI SRIVASTAVA

KALPAZ

First Published, 2018

Published by

Kalpaz Publications
C-30, Satyawati Nagar,
Delhi – 110052
E-mail: kalpaz@hotmail.com
Ph.: 9212142040

Printed at: G. Print Process, Delhi

Cataloging in Publication Data—DK
Courtesy: D.K. Agencies (P) Ltd. <docinfo@dkagencies.com>

Srivastava, Shivani *(Writer on dalit women)*, **author.**
A study on empowerment of scheduled caste women in Naugarh block of Chandauli District : a participatory approach / by Shivani Srivastava.
pages cm
"Thesis submitted for the degree of Doctor of Philosophy in Home Science (Extension education)."
ISBN 9789386397126

1. Rural women—Government policy—India—Naugarh (Block) 2. Dalits—Government policy—India—Naugarh (Block) 3. Women in rural development—India—Naugarh (Block) 4. Participatory rural appraisal—India—Naugarh (Block) I. Title.

LCC HQ1742.S65 2017 | DDC 305.4209542 23

This Book to be Dedicated to

My Father

Sri Indra Dev Srivastava

CONTENTS

INTRODUCTION

Chapter - 1

Introduction

"We are convinced that it is essential to design, implement and monitor, with the full participation of women, effective, efficient and mutually reinforcing gender sensitive policies and programmes, including development policies and programmes at all levels that will foster the empowerment and advancement of women"

— Platform for Action and the Beijing Declaration, 1995

Women Constitute one-half of the segment of pluralism in India. The 1991 census counted 495.7 millions females against a total population of 846.3 million, in which 207.8 millions women live in the rural areas and 27 per cent of the rural women live below the poverty line[1]. Scheduled caste and Schedule tribes share 16.48 and 8.08 per cent respectively in the total population of India[2]. These sections are among the poorest of the poor in the country even after more than half-a-century of planned economic and social development specially spelt out for their betterment[3]. It has been reported that majority of women in India residing in rural areas fall below poverty line and are engaged in agriculture, their life being characterised by drudgery, hard work and inadequate basic amenities[4], Discrimination of women from womb to tomb is well known. A great gender disparity can be observed in almost all sections of human life, especially in the areas of health, education and employment.

The lower sex ratio, low literacy rate, economic dependence, malnutrition, poor health status and low participation in decision-making process are few indicators, which highlight the pathetic status of women in India. In the UN's Human Development Report, (1995). India ranks 99th on Gender Related Development Index of 130 nations. The Gender Empowerment Measure which estimates the extent of women's participation in a country's economic and political activities, ranks India as 110th of the 116 nations. The report has identified the three crucial areas i.e. access to education, reproductive health and credit resources where women lag behind[5].

Government's Initiative to Achieve Women Empowerment

The prevailing gender biasness in Indian society has compelled the policy-makers to frame and implement specific programmes targeted towards the fair sex of the society in order to upgrade their social and economic status. Falling in line with the same objective, the United Nations Organisation has rightly declared the year 2001 as "Women Empowerment" year. The gender disparity in India is more pronounced in rural areas as compared to urban areas. This is primarily because of the problem of illiteracy and social backwardness among women.

The Year 2001 was declared as the Women's Empowerment Year by the Government of India. A task force on women and children was set up under the chairmanship of the Deputy Chairman, Planning Commission in Aug. 2000. The national policy for the empowerment of women has been approved by the cabinet in March 2001. The policy prescribes strategies and action points to bridge the gap between the equal dejure status and unequal de-facto position of women of the country.

It also seeks to guide action at every level and in every sectors by mainstreaming gender perspectives into all laws, policies, programmes, regulations and budget allocations of the government. A major strategy adopted during the Ninth Plan (1997-2002) has been to introduce a Women's Component Plan (WCP) under which not less than 30 per cent of the funds/ benefits should be specifically earmarked for women's programmes in all the women related sectors.

The major policy initiatives undertaken by the government in the recent past for welfare of women include inter-alia, restructuring of Indira Mahila Yojana (IMY), Balika Samridhi Yojana (BSY), Rural Women's Development and Empowerment Project (RWDEP), setting up of National Commission for Women (NCW), adoption of National Nutrition Policy and Rashtriya Mahila Kosh. The Indira Mahila Yojana launched in 1995-96, has been recast after merging Mahila Samridhi Yojana (MSY) and has been renamed as "Swayam Siddha" in 2001. It aims to empower women through awareness generation," achievement of economic strength, through micro-level income generating activities and establish convergence of various services such as health literacy, rural development etc. Rural Women's Development and Empowerment Project (RWDEP) now called as "Swa-Shakti Project", sanctioned in Oct. 1998, as a centrally sponsored project is aimed to create an environment for empowerment of women in the six states viz: Bihar, Haryana, Karnataka, Gujarat, Madhya Pradesh and Uttar Pradesh[6]. Indian Women's Economic Programme (IWEP) aims at organising women in Self Help Groups (SHGs) to form a strong institutional base. The schedule is being implemented in 238 community Development Blocks and more than 42,000 women Self Help Groups were formed by the end of year 2000. For encouraging employment and income generation, the programme for Support of Training and Employment (STEP) provides a comprehensive package of upgradation of skills through training, extension of inputs and market linkages in the traditional sectors of agriculture, dairying, handicrafts etc. The Socio-Economic Programmes (SEPs) which were launched, provide for work and 'wages to needy women such as destitute, widows etc. The Condensed Courses of Education and Vocational Training (CC and VT) provide new vistas of employment through continuing education and vocational training for school dropouts.

The Rashtriya Mahila Kosh (RMK) is a national level mechanism to meet the micro credit needs of the poor and assetless women in the informal sector. From inception in 1993 till Feb. 2001, total credit worth ₹ 100 crore was sanctioned to benefit more than 400,000 women through 827 NGOs, spread over the country. RMK has a very creditable recovery rate of 90 to 95 per cent. It has also ventured to develop an institutional base at grass roots level with the establishment of Self-Help Groups for expanding its credit services. Other beneficiary programmes of similar type include Integrated Child Development Scheme (ICDS), programme of providing Hostels for Working Women (HWW) and Short Stay Homes (SSH)[7]

Despite continuous allocations by the government to the above mentioned projects and a persistent effort to upgrade the socio-cconomic and health condition of women, much still remains to be achieved.

A World Bank report on Women's health status in India, released in 1996, has grimly catalogued the variety of ways in which women are discriminated against. Females in India generally get improper vaccination, less education and less nutrition than their male counterparts and when they grow up, they are less healthy than the males and succumb more easily to sickness and diseases. Women in rural areas, because of their household responsibilities and out of ignorance, tend to neglect their illness and hence fail to perform their household chores. The intra-household distribution of labour and resources are loaded against the girls, who work more and get a lesser share of food, healthcare and leisure. Poverty makes the situation all the more worse[8].

As far as education is concerned, the Govt. of India has reiterated its commitment towards the promotion of female education not only through the constitutional provisions but also through plans, policies and various programmes launched at block and village level at different points of time. Notwithstanding all the efforts put in by various organisations, literacy rate of women has so far remained quite low. The 1991 census data estimated female literacy in rural areas as 30.62 per cent as against 40.05 per cent in urban areas. Further, the literacy level of Scheduled Castes and Scheduled Tribes in rural areas were only 19.46 and 16.02 per cent respectively. It is an undeniable fact that involvement in household activities and child labour have largely kept girl child in rural areas away from the school.

As far as adult education for women is concerned, family work burden, shyness, traditional taboos, resistance from family members and preoccupation with child rearing activities have largely restricted them from acquiring education in educational centres[9].

The 1991 National Sample Survey figures show that women share only 14.1 per cent of employment to total employment. Moreover, it has also been revealed that the women labour force participation rate in rural areas is 33.1 per cent as against 16.2 per cent in urban area. The poverty and economic necessity have put women, particularly belonging to scheduled castes and scheduled tribes and other backward and economically weaker sections of the rural society, in unskilled and menial works requiring more labour hours for which they earn a partly sum. According to an ILO report released in 1992, women put more hours of work than men but invariably earn less than half of what men are paid. It 'further revealed that the employment which women get is irregular, uncertain, seasonal and discretionary and is characterised by mal practice in payment and non-repayment of wages[10].

The pathetic socio-economic condition of weaker section women can be observed from the Report of Govermnent of India, presented at the fourth World Conference on Women, Beijing (1995).

It states that two to three million people in the forest and tribal belts of India earn their livelihood by head loading. Of these, 90 per cent are women who walk long distances to sell loads of wood. Despite the harsh nature of work, many women have taken to it in the last two decades, as it is only work available round the year. Collection of minor forest produce and herbs have traditionally provided extra income, valuable nutrition and medicinal support. Their unability to readily access this due to retreating forest cover, has impoverished women without suitable alternatives. Being a part of labour-intensive and non-monetised economy, they have become victims of profiteers, middle men and also men in their families and communities[11].

Concept of Women Empowerment

Webster's II New Riverside University Dictionary and Furk and College Wagnalls Canadian Dictionary has defined the verb "Empowerment" as "To invest with legal power", "to authorise" and "to enable".

The concept of empowerment is related with concept of freedom. It refers to "equipping one self to improve her/his living condition"[12]. The term is operationally concerned with women empowerment. It is a multidimensional process which enables an individual or a group to establish their identity in all spheres of life[13]. Empowerment is the surest way of making women participant in the development process. In order that women accept the change and contribute fully to development, it is essential to develop first their potentiality by improving their knowledge, attitude and skills with as much concern for long run consequences as for short term gains[14].

In grass-root programmes and policy debates alike, "empowerment" has virtually replaced the terms such as welfare, upliftment, community participation and poverty alleviation to describe the goal of development and intervention[15]. "Empowerment" provides the key solution to many social problems like high population growth rates, environmental degradation, low status of women etc. The concept of women's empowerment appears to be the end result of a number of important discussion, dialogues and debates generated by the women's movements across the world". In India, the word empowerment" has been used widely in recent official pronouncement on the status of women. The Eighth and Ninth Five Year Plans have repeatedly highlighted the need for women upliftment[17].

In the Indian context, the empowerment issue is considered as one of the methodology through which efforts are made to integrate women with the development process by means of participatory development programmes on one side and development of their capacity of absorb inputs on the other[18].

Participatory Approach to Women Empowerment

Empowerment ofwomen can operationally be done through ideas, through consciousness and through education. They can be empowered not merely through social upgradation and economic betterment, but more specifically, through enhanced participation of all women with full support and assistance of men in the decision-making process of family and the community as a whole. Participation of women may include active involvement in microlevel planning, choice of vocations and training, formation of groups at their own will, greater access to most developmental programmes, access to credit facilities, education and health services and so on[19].

In the past, developmental projects were designed without the involvement of the intended beneficiaries and as a result they failed. The planning agencies have now realised the need to incorporate participatory principles into their projects. Consultations among NGOs prior to the 1992 UN Conference on Environment and Development (UNCED) identified five participatory criterias for sustainable development; who initiates? who decides? who participates? who benefits? and who controls? It was reported that the answer to all these question, was "people" including proportionate representation of women[20]. However, something more than participation was required and the term "empowerment" was coined which is operationally concerned with women upliftment. This "empowerment" can be frequently stimulated through Participatory Rural Appraisal (P.R.A.) exercise giving women, a clear sense of how they can improve their lives in a practical way[21].

Concept of P.R.A. and It's Relevance as Tool to Women Empowerment

It is now an established fact that for success of any rural development programme, P.R.A. is an important entry activity. The exercise is conducted to establish rapport with the village community as well as identify and define problems for prioritisation in the village itself. Based on principle of listening and learning, P.R.A. is the technique of immediate analysis and survey of village resources for participatory micro-planning and development[22].

P.R.A. is a means of generating different kinds of data, identifying and mobilising the intended groups and evoking their participation. It provides an alternative frame-work for data collection and analysis[23]. This depends upon the intimate knowledge of the community about local resources and empowers them for decision making[24]. P.R.A. has got the ability to empower both, those who, through P.R.A., express and share what they already know, learn through that expression and sharing and those who investigate and observe add to their knowledge and become more aware about the local conditions. Various P.R.A. tools are available to suit this task i.e., empowerment. Such tools include participatory mapping, household listing, well-being ranking, livelihood analysis, focus group discussion, social and resource mapping etc[25]. The importance of perceptions of rural women can hardly be overemphasised. Their role in society, problems, priorities and capabilities, if truly appreciated through this method can lay the foundations of a gender based approach to rural development[26].

Statement of the Problem

The study was conducted in a remote area i.e. Naugarh block of Chandauli district. The block Naugarh is thickly dominated by Kharwar (a tribe) caste comprising 60 per cent of total population with varying percentage of other caste like Musahar, Yadav, Chamar, Baniya and Brahmins. The block is spread in around 211 square km. area, of which 60 per cent is covered with hillock and forest. Total population of the block is 452006 as per 1991 census. (23856 male and 21334 female) spread in 111 (one hundred and eleven) villages. Overall literacy of the block is 22 per cent, women are at the worst edge having literacy of only 5 per cent.

Like many other settlements in forest and hilly regions of India, the women of Naugarh block work hard and devote maximum time and energy in agriculture and livestock management along with household activities like cleaning of house, clothes, utensils, cooking meal, maternal care, collecting fuel, fodder and water from distant forests etc. Data collected in this regard (1993) reveal that in cultivation of one hectare of paddy and wheat, women devote 1928 hrs. while men 796 hrs. and a pair of bullock 896 hrs[27]. The women contribute more in food production than men but they fail to get due recognition in the society. They do not participate in decision making related to household activities. The Panchayati Raj Institutions have provided women an opportunity to participate in political and decision-making process, but she failed to get adequate social and political encouragement.

The above situation calls for a conducive environment in which women can share their experiences and participate in finding solutions to their problems and needs and set priorities to handle such problems.

Keeping in mind the aforementioned problems of the women of Naugarh block of Chandauli district, the present study was conducted with participatory approach under which local women were enabled to analyse their living conditions, to share their problems and to plan their activities. The objectives of the study were as follows.

Objectives

1. To know the socio-personal characteristic of women in the area.
2. To know about the gender perception of women in the area.
3. To know the health, hygiene and sanitation condition of women in the area.
4. To identify their problems/needs and to classify them in order of priority.
5. To plan, implement and evaluate a participatory intervention programme for women empowerment.

The study was conducted through P.R.A. (Participatory Rural Appraisal) method which has an inbuilt mechanism to encourage participation and empowerment of local people (especially women) during study period by:

– Investigating local insights gained by interfacing with the common man, resulting in more effective "research information" being located[28].

– Involving local people in research and design of socio-economic endeavours so as to lead to increasing commitment and empowerment of local people[29].

Hypothesis of the Study

1. Women in the area have an innate ability to create knowledge.
2. Investigation is an educational process for the participants as well as the researcher.

Justification of the Study

The present study is exploratory, interactive and participatory in nature. Participatory Rural Appraisal is an emerging method of advocating women empowerment, hence the proposed research may prove to be an eye opener for the policy-makers and organisations, dealing with women empowerment in following ways.

1. It will direct the efforts being made for the empowerment of women preferably in case of women in difficult and risk-prone environment.
2. It will accelerate the process of women empowerment and encourage women participation in enhancing self-esteem and confidence among them.
3. The study area falls in the central plateau, thus having a possibility of wide scope replication.
4. It will bring about appropriate and conducive environment for defining women empowerment.
5. Last but not the least, it will pave the path for women empowerment process with in the reality of area.

REVIEW OF LITERATURE

Chapter - 2

Review of Literature

Literature on women studies is voluminous. It embraces all walks of women's life. However, the thrust is uniformly the same - the inferior status of women in one form or the other, under various pretexts, and their consequences.' Present chapter involves review of literature available, which are related to the following categories:

(a) Women in Development Programmes.

(b) Socio-economic and health status of rural women.

(c) P.R.A. studies related to gender issues.

(a) Women in Development Programmes

Women development is directly related to national development. A large number of programmes have been initiated for women's development. These programmes lay emphasis on providing equal opportunities to women by removing gender-bias, empowering women and creating self reliance. It stresses on adoption of a holistic approach to women's development encompassing health, education and employment.[30]

Shakuntala Narsimham has precisely analysed in the book "Empowering Women" that the women still possess lower status even after fifty years of planned development. She further states that "For the first 25 years of development planning in India, it was assumed that the development made by the population as a whole, would ultimately be shared by all sections, and that whatever benefits accrued to the men would also percolate to the women and result in better status and gender equality. This, however, turned out to be a faulty assumption, as periodic assessments at the end of each plan period revealed.

In 1971, the government appointed a commission on the status of women in India. Its report, "Towards equality", led to debates that highlighted the need to view women not just as targets of welfare policies, but also as 'critical actors of development'. However, the planners' approach remained largely unchanged, and by the end of the Fourth Five Year Plan (1969-74), it was clear that the growth effect was not trickling down to the weaker sections of the population, including women, scheduled castes and scheduled tribes.

A Minimum Needs Programme was therefore incorporated in the Fifth Plan model. However, the household continued to be targeted as the beneficiary, the approach itself was based on the concept of patriarchy. There was no mention of women's specific needs in the areas listed for priority attention under the programme.

The Sixth Plan document began, again, with an admission that the weaker sections (SCs/STs, women and the rural poor) were still lagging behind in terms of incremental development.[31]

Likewise, the report of the commissioner for scheduled castes and scheduled tribes (1975-77) observed that -

"Perhaps the effort made so far to change the milieu by state action have been more in the nature of expedients rather than borne out by a firm conviction to change the social landscape, to initiate a social revolution whatever the social and political costs the transition might demand.[32]

By the end of Fifth Plan, an expenditure of ₹ 3,410 million had been incurred for SCs but mostly in terms of adhoc subsidies, grants and tokenism. No permanent solutions came out of that exercise, and the Sixth Plan began with the country having a larger population of poor than the entire population at the time of independence three decades earlier (361 million). Independent studies concluded that the fruits of economic development had been appropriated mostly by the top 2030 per cent of the population rather than those for whom they were meant.

A chapter on women and development was included for the first time, in the Sixth Plan document. Targeting rural poor women in particular, the plan declared that, 'a fair share of employment opportunities would have to be created through poverty alleviation programmes'. The assumption continued to be that employment and income generation would automatically lead to improvements in the status of women.

This belief, as the policy-makers themselves were to concede subsequently, was simplistic. The two plans that followed noted that the results of developmental efforts in terms of both poverty alleviation and improvements in the status of women had not been commensurate with the inputs made.[33]

A separate ministry for women and child development was created in 1984. In the Seventh Five Year Plan, the Planning Commission moved further away from the "welfare" approach of the Sixth Plan to a more positive "developmental" approach to women's concerns. The Indian Parliament adopted a 'National Policy on Education - 1986' which included a chapter on 'Education for Women's equality'. The Government of India launched the

"Twenty-Point Programme" in 1975 pinpointing areas of special thrust. The programme has been subsequently recast and refined in 1982 and in 1986 with equality for women as a thrust area.[34] The Seventh Five Year Plan of development programmes for women had a major objective of raising their economic and social status. In the Eighth Five Year Plan, there was a definite shift from development to empowerment of women. The Ninth Five Year Plan document has declared empowerment of women as one of the nine primary objectives. The commitments of the Ninth Plan (1997-2002) envisages the empowering of women as the agents of social change and development.[35]

Over the past many years, development programmes have largely yielded somewhat disappointing results. Efforts have been planned and carried out almost entirely by and for men, with little concern for the role of women. Any effort that overlooks half the people involved obviously leads to a failure. Hence, "many development planners now realise that the full participation of women in development directly involves, half the available human resources, holds, the greatest potential for break-throughs in many difficult sectors, and offers the key to unlock the development dilemma".[36]

Various studies emphasising integration of women with development programmes have been depicted as under :

M.S. Swaminathan in his lecture in 1982, at Centre for Women's Development Studies, New Delhi concluded that to obtain a correct perception of priorities, there is a need for direct integration between scientists and women farmers. Policy-makers will have to listen and learn from resource poor rural women. He further says that women as well as men, both need to be educated. Since many of the current difficulties stemup from differing perceptions of men and women, whether with regard to family planning or sanitation or social forestry or drinking water supply, it would be important to convince both of them for the success of any development programmes regarding above aspects.[37]

The concept of women development requires broader definition and clearer understanding. Development implies not merely social upgradation and economic betterment, but more specifically, enhanced participation of all women with full support and assistance of men in the family and the community as a whole. Participation of women may include active involvement in micro-level planning, choice of vocations and training, formation of group at their own free will, greater access to most development programmes available in the community, access to credit, know how, education, nutrition and health services and so on.[38]

Kashyap and Gupta emphasised the need for appropriate strategy for poverty alleviation by stressing involvement of the people for whom the programme is meant.[39] The need for focus on women participation in development strategy was stressed by the United Nations Development Decades as "It goes without saying that women integration in development is a gradual process that, in the end, will benefit not only women, but the whole society of men, women and children". Any policy regarding improving food security, economic betterment etc need greater political support and farmers, (specially women), must be recognised as the main stakeholders. There is a need to continuously work towards understanding their condition, priorities and constraints and to do something to try and improve their situation.[40]

Significant difference was observed between women who had been exposed to the awareness generation strategy and women who have not been exposed to awareness generation. In other words, instead of imposing decisions on them as the conventional strategy assume, the decisions come from women themselves in the form of their own perception and conventions.[41]

(b) Socio-economic and Health Status of Rural Women

Women's condition in any society is an index of the civilisation among the people. Rural women of lower caste are exploited and deprived of by their poverty, illiteracy, ill health of means to escape from a short life of drudgery and fatigue.[42] Woman's role in economic development is an integral part of rural life and their invisibility as an economic entity is at the root of her low status. Cultural system of rural India still views man as the primary bread winner.[43] The level of income, education, employment, health and social status of the family to which one belongs are certain parameters which reflect the family and community, as per the conclusion of the study 'Involvement of females in decision-making process in rural sectors of parts of 'Thar desert' by Tiwari. She further says that the poor involvement of concerned female members in decision making process related to family management affairs in rural population also determines their low status in the society.[44]

Rural women mostly do, not only their household chores, but also a number of farm activities. The arduous tasks like field preparations, manuring and fertiliser application, irrigating the crops and construction and repair of the field channels are still the monopoly of men folk. Besides, there are several other activities which involves joint work as transplantation, FYM (Farm Yield Manure) making, weeding operations, harvesting the crops, storage of farm produce and marketing of live stocks. In these activities, women play supporting role with men counterparts.[45] Women work also consist of collecting fuel and fetching water.[46] They maintain kitchen garden, orchards, poultry, dairy etc. They are better, silent forces available at village who perform unpaid works effectively for the cause of the welfare of the community as a whole. Inspite of all these it is an irony that women are unable to free themselves from the dominance of men as they do not have enough finance and courage to operate independently.[47] A critical reason for non-recording of women's work is that it is to a large extent labelled as domestic work and this is conventionally excluded from statistically recognised work. The exclusion is particularly misleading as it concerns rural women's work in developing countries where it often includes all post-harvest processing of grains and the fetching of water and fuel. in addition to child care, cooking and other household duties.[48]

According to 1991 census, the male cultivators have increased in the country by 11.67 per cent from 7.67 crore in 1981 to 8.56 crore in 1991. The female cultivators, however, increased at a much faster rate from 1.48 crore in 1981 to 2.15 crore in 1991. The number of male agricultural labourers increased by 31.48 per cent. 74 per cent of entire female working force is engaged in agricultural operations; 28 per cent as cultivators and 46 per cent as agricultural labourers. About 60 per cent of agricultural operations like sowing of seeds, transplanting of saplings, winnowing, storage of grains etc. are handled almost exclusively by women while in other jobs, they share the work with men.[49]

A few of the studies indicating the contribution of rural women in agriculture are as following:

A study by Dak50 conducted in four districts of Haryana with 160 respondents from four villages found widespread participation of women in agricultural activities. In nearly half of the activities concerned, women are playing a dominant role.

The level of women participation in family affairs and farm activities were the major objectives of a study by Shobha.[51] Primary datas were collected from four villages of two districts in the Telangana region of Andhra Pradesh on the basis of random stratifying sampling method. The analysis showed that though the participation of female agricultural labourers was dominant in many activities, they were not recognised properly due to traditional socio-economic conditions, superiority feelings of male family members and lack of self-organisation of women.

The objective of a paper by Singh[52] was to study the degree of involvement of women in farm and family work and to quantify the impact of new technology on employment and decision making. From 21 villages of Almora district of the then undivided Uttar Pradesh, 144 families were randomly selected as the sample for the study. On an average, three-fourth of the "total work in agriculture was performed by the female members of the family". Men were playing dominant role in decision making. Impact of innovation and improved technology regarding agriculture was less known among women because of their illiteracy and less decision making power.

The study entitled[54] Agricultural Modernisation and Third World Women analysed the effect of agricultural modernisation on women. The study is based on data from Tamil Nadu and Andhra Pradesh. It was observed that : (a) rural women work for longer hours than men; (b) distribution of food within the family tended to favour men; (c) men controlled income; (d) female headed households increased; and (e) women tend to lose more from a scheme than the men of their class.

A study "on women's involvement in wheat and paddy cultivation in Haryana" observed that women performed 90 per cent of head-load work and weeding and about 65 per cent of harvesting. Tasks which were less drudgery-ridden were assigned to men. There was greater need for educational rather than technological programme to emancipate women in agriculture.

The role and participation of women in agriculture production system in the villages of coastal West Bengal were studied" and it was found that women were fully responsible for fruits and vegetable production in homestead farming. A study[56] about the role of women in agriculture was conducted in Orissa with a sample size of 404 farm families. The study highlighted that women played a significant role in agricultural activities and existing extension system was not sufficient to offer farming information to women. Tribal women also do important farming operations and participate with men in all major decisions in the family.

The objective of the study by Banu[57] was to find out the role of women in livestock production and the result showed that the role of women was highly significant in rural families. Women participation and productivity are found to be high in animal husbandry than in any other agricultural activity.

Regarding Health Status of Women, it may be rightly concluded that it is basic pre-condition to their advancement. The fundamental issues concerning women and their health are nutrition, sanitation, infection, over work, mental tensions, pregnancy, early marriage and reproductive phase. In 1991, the sex ratio registered was 927 female per thousand males. The main reason for this declining sex ratio is high mortality rate among females in all age groups. In rural areas, women are overburdened with the households as well as the outdoor jobs. As shown in the studies above, it may be unanimously concluded that these multifarious activities resulted in poor health and low nutritional status of women. Food consumption is affected by the availability of agricultural commodities, occupational status, income, family composition, habits and tradition. This, in turn, determines the health profile of rural women.[58] There is substantial maternal mortality and anaemia among pregnant and lactating mothers due to poor nutrition. There is also a tendency not to report female ailments or seek medical aid. Child-bearing and high fertility impose additional health problems for women. Limited water and sanitation facilities not only do affect women's own health, but also prevent them from effective performance of essential tasks within the households.[59]

Literature regarding discrimination in education, extension and technology are being reviewed as under :

Education, extension and training will enrich and empower women. Technology will equip them in acquiring new skills and to lessen their drudgery.

It is widely known that the present high illiteracy among women is one of the major constraints in their scope of employment and social status. Educating women has greater multiplier effect than educating men.[60] Buxi[61] is of the opinion that literacy alone can make women realise their potential and equip them for better employment and wages. The sex-wise educational imbalance impair women's contribution to development. By imparting technical and general education to women, their status can be improved.[62] Discrimination against women in education and employment opportunities systematically excludes them from participatory growth.

Despite the important role of women in agriculture; agricultural programmes hardly benefit them.[63] All programmes of transfer of technology in agriculture tend to bypass women which deprive them the status of skilled labourers and to get rightful return.[64]

P.R.A. Studies Related to Gender Issues

(Some of the studies emphasising thc participation of women in development and research process and P.R.A. studies related to data collection regarding gender issues has been reviewed as under :

Jyotipati Durba[65] has given the basic logic for the success of any intervention in any development work. He says that the amount of schemes and projects do not count, but what matters is the peoples' decision and community initiatives. He describes eight point principles which one should follow for development and research. (1) Go to the people, (2) Live among them, (3) Learn from them, (4) Love them, (5) Serve them, (6) Plan with them, (7) Start with what they know and (8) Build on what they have.

Robert Chamber[66] a well known person in the field of participatory research, argues while asking "what is relevant information and how to get it's reliability?" He says that participatory approach is rather better than a survey approach of research. P.R.A. is based on participation with the concerned community/group/people. Its approach lies more on realising local people's capabilities and their long term view on sustainability. Outsider is only a catalyst facilitating them in the process of development. Rigour of relevance is more important than rigour of measurement. P.R.A. distinguishes itself from other approaches by shared visual representation and allowing locals to analyse themselves. Success of P.R.A. rests on three pillars; behaviour and attitudes, methods and sharing and partnership (between locals and outsiders).

Participatory Rural Appraisal techniques of social investigation involve full participation of the community; an educational process and a means of taking action for development. It is a research structured by the democratic interaction of the researcher and oppressed classes of people.

This section seeks to illustrate gender aspects of rural life based on learning from field experiences. It focuses on rural women and brings out different aspects of their life. The methodology applied is that of P.R.A. related to gender analysis and reflect various aspects such as expertise and role in selected activities, nature of work and daily routine, their deprivation through food discrimination and their ranking of problems and prioritisation.

A study was conducted in hamlet Zhagdhar tribal village in Thane District of Maharashtra. The hamlet consist of 48 households, most of which belong to groups of small and marginal farmers and landless labourers. The villagers formed two groups of 12 to 15 each - one group of women and the other of men. They were asked to prepare village maps depicting different households, roads, water bodies and other structures. One major point of difference was the omission of footpaths in men's map. One reason to explain the difference was to do with the relevance of roads and footpaths to men and women. The footpaths were being daily used by the village women for collection of fuelwood, fodder and water.

Adams, A.R., Das Roy, *et.al.*[67] in their joint project undertaken in Jamalpur, Bangladesh tried to identify indigenous indicators of health, wealth and women's status and to investigate people's perceptions of changes in these indicators over time. The time line and focus group discussion about change showed particularly how women felt after having greater influence in household decision-making, due to involvement in credit and training programme. The indigenous indicators of women status chosen varied according to whether women were project beneficiaries or not.

Bilgi, M.[68] stated in his study that P.R.A. activities were conducted in Gujarat with group of village women, with men observing in the backgroup. The women counted the number of families in each caste and class-wise distribution of farmers, then used circles to construct a chart showing their debts. Finally, they estimated how many hours they spent on various activities each day, using twigs on a chart.

Another study of Bilgi, M.[69] at Boripitha, (Netrang), P.R.A. activity estimating women's time use was carried out with a group of men who had resisted improved technologies for domestic work.

Through identifying the different activities a woman does in a day, men are amazed to find that the total time worked is 19 hours. The actual conversation between the participants and trainer is reported, as they go on to discuss whether women's work can easily be compared to men's.

Francis S., J. Devaram *et al.,*[70] in their project work have described that a topical PRA on health was held in South India for 23 participants belonging to 11 NGO groups. Activities were conducted separately by the NOG group and women's group : their different perceptions of health problems were compared on a table. Information on the reproduction cycle was also produced by the women's group. Some general observation made about women's participation include: 'women have come out with seasonal calendar of ten months'.

Study of Gujeet, I.,[71] concludes that for producing a series of audio visual material for change, agents working in co-operation with farmer's group and in natural resource projects generated the topics to be covered and P.R.A. tools for gender analysis. Semi-structured interviews with key-informants and focus group could form the basis of all interaction with local men and women and acquired the informations regarding gender roles in forest management, water, soil and agriculture management.

This collection of P.R.A. activities used for gender analysis IS supplemented by maps, diagrams and calendar drawn by women and men from a variety of countries. Aknowledge of P.R.A. technique is needed as there is little written explanation with the illustration.[72]

Another study by Gujeet, I.,[73] suggests that P.R.A. is not automatically gender sensitive - there is a need to raise gender awareness first before P.R.A. tools can be used to explore different perceptions and it is not enough simply to say that gender is important.

Hadded *et at.*[74] reported that to explore P.R.A. as a research tool for generating indicators in the context of large quantitative survey, four field exercise were carried out in India. Village mapping activity identified the households at 'very high risk' or 'no risk' as defined by the villagers and conducted separately for men and women in order to measure gender differentiated of risk.

Jonfa, E., *et al.*[75] described in their study that participatory modelling was organised by a team on a training course in North Umo. To avoid men from dominating in the activity, as is usual, only one group was formed. The group was sub-divided into men, women and children. Each sub-group created a model which showed their different perception and the areas of interventions.

Krishna Murthy, R.,[76] described the process of training at community level, showing that the existing P.R.A. methods have been used to help raise gender awareness. (e.g. ranking according to oppression, not just wealth and social mapping to show gender based ownership).

Sahu[77] stated that a P.R.A. exercise was carried out to analyse the positive and negative effects of drinking in a tribal area of India. Casual diagrams were produced of drinking habits and women's status, showing the different consequences of birth of a female child as compared to male child.

Tolly, E., *et al.,*[78] stressed to adapt some of the participatory methods developed within agriculture for conducting P.R.A. exercise on women's health.

A body mapping exercise was conducted with a group of traditional birth attendants to discuss their concepts of reproduction, contraception and nutrition. A village mapping exercise led later to construction of 'pregnancy time lines' and information on family planning acceptors.

The Women Development Project (W.D.P.) of CARE Bangladesh trains women in 441 villages as local health educators. A mapping exercise was conducted in a village in langail with 13 of these women. In three neighbourhood groups, the women drew maps using sticks and flour, showing the households that they worked with and which new health practices they had adopted.[79]

Wellbourn, A.,[80] describes that P.R.A. methods can help us to counter - the assumption that rural-communities are fairly homogeneous groups of people. P.R.A. can be used as a method for identifying, exploring and analysing intra-communal difference and as a means of training development workers. The gender examples show the different results of certain P.R.A. exercise when attempted by men and women separately on seasonal calendars, women would always include childhood diseases and were better at identifying individual disease patterns. When asked to draw changes on a map, women complained that the kind of changes we need can't be drawn (wife beating, over work).

From the literature cited above on women studies, it may be concluded that there is no dispute among academicians or policy-makers that women in rural areas are possessing the lower socio-economic and health status.

It is unfortunate that women are not target group for input of modern innovation and research. Mere identification of women as target group does not serve the purpose of rural women. It is of paramount importance to ensure their participation at all levels of implementation of programmes. It is possible only when she herself expresses her problems and needs and develops a participatory programme for her own upliftment. Attempts have been initiated in this area with the acceptance of the participatory approach of research and development. Non Governmental Organisations are doing their best in this regard. Present study is an attempt to identify the problems/needs of women by sharing their feelings and to collect the data regarding desired objectives.

RESEARCH METHODOLOGY

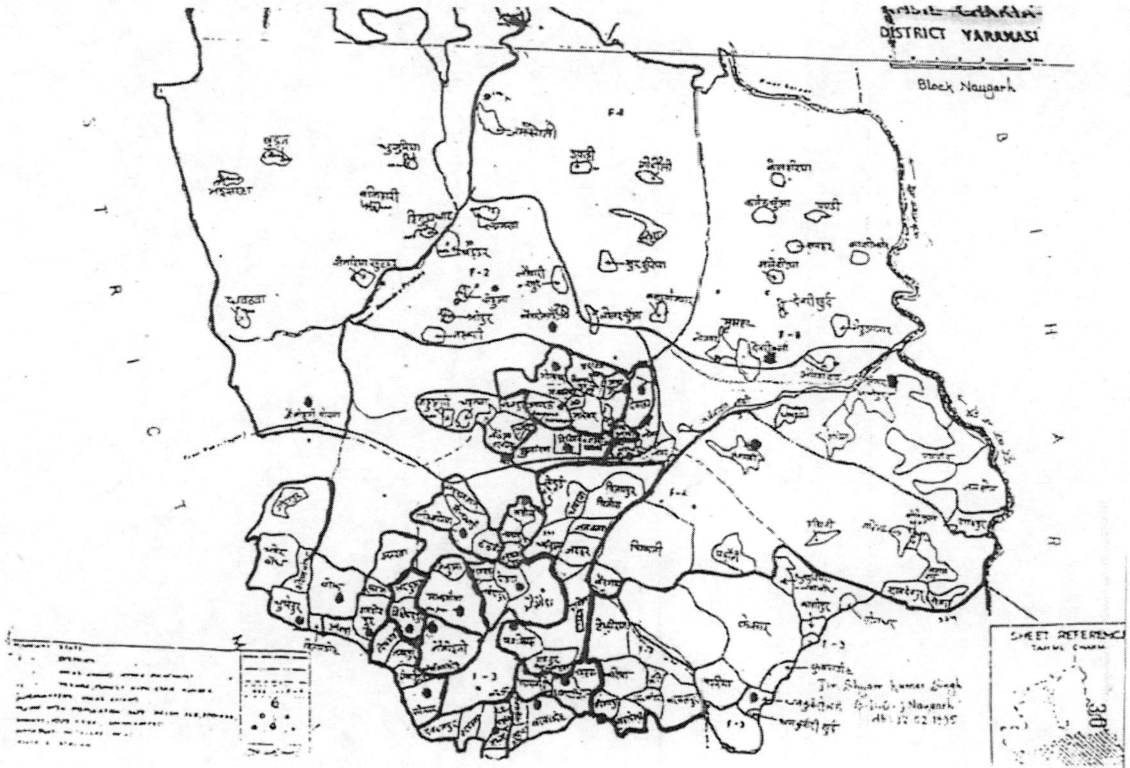
DISTRICT VARANASI
Block Naugarh
B
I
H
A
R
S
T
R
I
C
T
SHEET REFERENCE
30°

Chapter - 3

Research Methodology

For accuracy and success of any investigation, application of scientific methodology is necessary as it directly affects the authenticity of research findings. This chapter has been devoted to the presentation and discussion of methods and techniques employed to explore the possible explanation of objectives laid down for the study. Presenting the relevant aspects, this chapter has been organised in the following heads :-

1. Locale of the study.
2. Selection of the villages.
3. Selection of respondents.
4. Data collection.
5. Methods and techniques used in field enquiry.
6. Theoretical conceptualisation about Participatory Rural Appraisal (P.R.A.).

Locale of the Study

The study was conducted in Naugarh block of Chandauli district. The area was selected purposely because of extensive weaker section i.e. SCs and STs population residing in the block. The block is bounded in the north by Varanasi district, in the east by Shahabad (Bihar), in south by Pargana Bijaygarh of Pargana of Barhar, Ahraua and Bhuilli. The block is spread in around 211 square km. area, of which 60 per cent part is covered with hillocks and forest cover. The forest area is constituted as reserve forest under the Indian Forest Act 1927.[81]

About 50 per cent population of the block belong to scheduled castes and scheduled tribe communities like Kharwar, Chero, Musahar, etc. who live enclose vicinity of the forest areas of Naugarh and Chakiya blocks. These tribal people are categorised into scheduled castes and scheduled tribes by the D.P. Govemment. The forests are mainly tropical, dry, mixed, deciduous type.

The vegetations growing in these forests play a vital role in the economy of these people.[82] The main occupation of the area is agriculture and animal husbandry. However, forest product collection and sale of the same gives them sufficient earnings. Average land holding (especially of SCs and STs) is around two acres, most of which is upland (60 per cent) with low fertility. Average annual income of a family consisting of two adults and four children varies between ₹ 10,000-15,000 which barely meets their family needs. Thus, most of the weaker section families virtually fall in debt trap by repeatedly taking institutional and non-institutional loans. Almost all families (7801) residing in the block posses similar socioeconomic status but weaker section families (4500, 57 per cent) are at the worst edge.[83]

Selection of Villages

Out of one hundred and eleven villages, six villages were selected randomly from the list of villages having more than 50 per cent scheduled castes population. The selection was made in consultation with block officials. Villages selected for the study were:-

1. Aurawantand
2. Semar
3. Nunwat
4. Musahar
5. Shahpur
6. Kannabandh

Selection of Respondents

As it was an interactive and participatory research, all women were targeted as respondents (Census sampling). Women were individually interviewed as well as motivated to participate in different P.R.A. sessions to gather informations for the purpose.

Data Collection

The study was conducted between July 1999 to June 2000. However, seasonal availability of women was also taken into account, as they were not available in monsoon season due to their extensive engagement in the fields.

Two visits in a month for 6-8 days were done for developing better rapport among women. Thus, researcher spent 16 days in a month in the block itself.

However, the local women's engagements in household or in agricultural farms affected the visit pattern, But the researcher tried to offset the seasonal and respondents bias in the study by gathering data in different seasons.

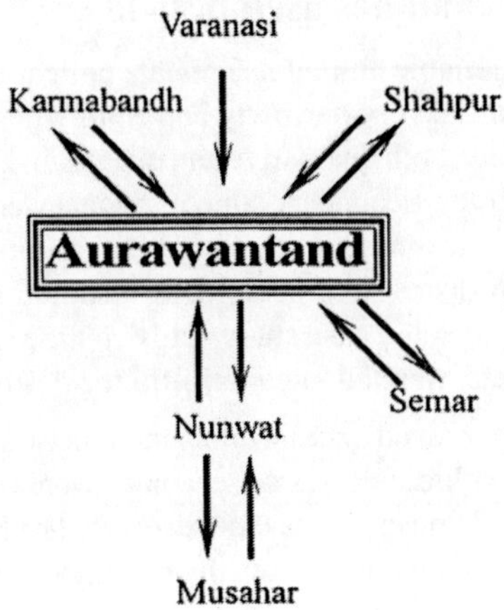

One Visit	-	Total 8 days
First two days	-	Nunwat and Musahar
2nd "	-	Shahpur
3rd "	-	Semar
4th "	-	Aurawantand and Karmabandh

Total 8 days in one visit.

Total 16 days in a month for period of 8 months (June 99 to May 2000)

The block is 90 Km. away from the Banaras Hindu University campus. Researcher was well acquainted with the local dialect, which exclusively benefited her to develop rapport with local women and understand their feelings and experiences. Aurawantand village was a centre ofa N.G.O. (N.C.D.C, National Communication Development Council) which was made as a base village, from where other villages were visited.

The data collection initiated with rapport building in various P.R.A. sessions in order to establish effective community dialogue. It was done in an open and relaxed manner through informal sittings with women group.

The researcher started a functional literacy programme on extensive demand of local women in the-area, which was followed by awareness generation programmes on different topics.

The effort proved to be a great success as there was enthusiastic participation and involvement of local women. Since the programme was conducted in local dialect, it was easily understood by them and consequently the researcher got a good response.

Methods / Techniques used in field enquiry

For a more reliable and intensive data collection, the researcher did not limit herself to those very narrowly and rigidly defined methods or tools of research. Therefore, both qualitative and quantitative data gathering tools were adopted in the survey. Secondary sources of data were also taken into account. Some quantitative techniques like sample survey and qualitative P.R.A. tools like focus group discussion, social and resource mapping, seasonal work calendars, food calendar, case study, daily routine chart, livelihood analysis, flow-diagrams, etc. were adopted to fulfill the desired objectives.

Tape recorder proved to be an unplanned successful tool to gather different data regarding their life styles, as these women were very much fond of listening their own recorded voices, in the tape recorder. The local songs, sung by these women reflected their feelings about their loneliness, poor economic condition, illiteracy, gender discrimination through which they undergo.

Theoretical conceptualisation about the participatory approach i.e. Participatory Rural Appraisal (P.R.A.)

Participatory Rural Appraisal (PRA) helps in interacting with local communities, for understanding and learning from them. It facilitates the process of involvement of local stake holders for harmonising with their indigenous knowledge. It is a way of learning from and working with community members to investigate, analyse and evaluate constraints and opportunities as well as to make to informal and timely decisions about development initiatives.

PRA involves a set of principles, process of communication and a menu of techniques for soliciting villagers' participation in putting forward their points of view about any issue and enabling them to do their own analysis as well as make contribution in different forms. This initiates a participatory process and sustains it[84].

1. Principles shared by P.R.A.

(i) A reversal of learning

To learn from rural people, directly, on the site, and face to face, gaining from local physical, technical and social knowledge.

(ii) Learning rapidly and progressively

With conscious exploration, flexible use of methods, opportunism, improvisation and cross-checking, not following a blueprint programme, but being adaptable in a learning process.

(iii) Offsetting biases

Specially those of rural development, by being relaxed and not rushing, listening not lecturing, probing instead of passing on to the next topic, being unimposing in approach to the problem, and seeking out to the poorer people and women, and learning about their concerns and priorities.

(iv) Optimising trade off

Relating to the costs of learning to the useful truth of information, with trade offs between quantity, relevance, accuracy and timeliness. This include the principle of optimal ignorance, knowing what is not worth-knowing, and of appropriate imprecision - not measuring more than needed. As Keynes is reputed to have said: "it is better to be approximately right than precisely wrong".

(v) Triangulating

Meaning using a range (sometimes three) of methods, types of information, investigators and/or disciplines to cross-check.

(vi) Seeking diversity

This has been expressed-in terms of seeking variability rather than averages and has been defined as maximising the diversity and richness of information.

(vii) Facilitating

They do it, facilitating investigation, analysis, presentation and learning by rural people themselves, so that they present and own the outcomes, and also learn[85].

2. The menu methods of P.R.A.

A summary listing of headings has been given below which gives the indication of types of methods used in the study.

(i) Secondary Sources

Such as reports, maps, articles and books.

(ii) Key Informants

Who are the experts; by seeking information from them.

(iii) Focus Group Discussion

Focus group discussion offer a means of obtaining in-depth information on a specific topic through a discussion group. The underlying premise is that people who share common experiences, problems or concerns are willing to reveal them in a group atmosphere.

(iv) Participatory mapping

People use ground, floor or paper to make social and demographic maps and to depict natural resource (Soils, trees, forests, water resources etc.) of their land.

(v) Transact walks

Systematically walking with informants through an area, observing, asking, listening, discussing, identifying different -zones, and seeking problems, solutions and opportunities.

(vi) Time Line

Chronologies of events, listing major remembered events in a village with approximate dates.

(vii) Seasonal Diagramming

By major season or by month, to show days and distribution of rain, crops, diet, food consumption, types of sickness, prices, animal fodder, fuel, income, debt etc.

(viii) Scoring and ranking

Especially using matrices and seeds to compare through scoring.

(ix) Participatory diagramming

Of flows, causality, impact, mobility, quantity, ranking and scoring, in which people make their own diagrams -bar diagrams, pie diagram. Chapati or Venn-diagramming is one from, a method for identifying individuals and institutions important in and for a community, and their relationship.

(x) Stories and Case studies

Such as household history and profile, coping with a crisis, how a conflict was or was not resolved.

3. Participatory Planning

In which villagers prepare their own plans, budgets and schedules and monitor progress[86].

Objective-wise description of tools and techniques along with their conceptual meanings are described on the next page.

Sl. No.	Issues	Concept	Tools and Techniques
1.	Socio-personal characteristic	It is defined as condition of women in society, ascertained by socio-personal characteristic variables like age, caste, education, income, type of house and land holding etc.	Questionnaire and livelihood analysis.
2.	Gender perception	It is the analysis of differences in perception of women, which can make differences in understanding rural issues.	Focus group routine charts discussion, Daily seasonal work calendar etc.
3.	Health hygiene and sanitation	It is the analysis of condition, problem, causes and related subject matter in area of health, hygiene and sanitation.	Focus group discussion, charts and maps prepared by women.prioritising ranking and scoring.
4.	Problems, needs and opportunities	It is to list out various problems, needs and priorities and rank it orderly.	

4. Cross-checking of data

Cross-checking is required to establish trust-worthiness of any study, to fill gaps and to improve the quality of the study. It was done through:-

- Triangulation.
- Participant observation.
- Checking with conventional survey data
- Peer-group checking.

RESULT AND DISCUSSION

PHOTO - 1

ATTEMPTS OF RAPPORT BUILDING AMONG WOMEN FOLK

Community Participation in a Ceremonial Function

Tape Recorder, An Important Tool, Was Used to Gather Women Folk at One Place and Create Interest About the Programme

the programme proved to be an important initiative to get closer to their lives. Several informations were gathered through their participation about their lives.

Objective-wise results and discussions are as follows :

OBJECTIVE ONE

Socio-Personal Characterstics of women

General Information abou t the respondents in selected villages

It may be recalled that for intensive field study, six villages were chosen. Namely:

1. Nunwat
2. Aurawantand
3. Musahar
4. Shahpurand
5. Semar
6. Karmabandh

Table 3 Distribution of respondents and their literacy status:

Regarding literacy of women, among six surveyed villages, few women (9) (out of 303) were found literate said they had some schooling (but not enough to be able to read). In terms of conventional schooling as a measure of education there was no significant difference between the respondents in the different groups of villages. This literacy was among the women of high caste (Brahmin) in Nunwat. Excluding five women of Kharwar caste all women were found illiterate.

Reason for the illiteracy of women in the areas was :- (1) traditional belief (2) typical agro ecological situation (3) lack of primary schools (4) Non-availability of primary school teachers (5) Poor transport facilities etc. One school situated in Nunwat village has got only one teacher who does not belong to the village itself. He faces difficulties of proper transportation facilities, proper accomodation, lack of drinking water and food items, which hinders him to come regularly to school.

What even may be the reasons behind low literacy rate among women, it has been observed that pow, girls of the area are being sent to the schools for education upto primary level. But the belief still looms large that a girl should be more perfect in household jobs rather than be highly educated. However, women themselves showed much interest to be literate in the participatory intervention programmes of functional literacy.

Chapter - 4

Result and Discussion: Rapport Building In practice

In a participatory framework, it is essential for a researcher to establish channels of effective-communication with local communities.

A number of frequent visit to women in the area with the objective of building communication links were done for the purpose of rapport building with such study villages. Initially, women were not willing to get associated. They asked that what will they get, by sharing their problems and feelings with the researcher. It was truely an ice breaking exercise and it took a very long time to convince these women.

Regarding socio-economic status, direct questioning about their age, caste, income, literacy status and land-holdings were done. Besides this participatory methods were also applied to analyse their livelihood condition. Participatory methods like mapping, do it yourself, ranking and scoring etc were used after developing an effective rapport with women folk and proved to gather the more reliable and valid data of their lives. P.R.A. is a process of participation with the respondents in which rapport building paves the way for them to perform their own analysis and to express themselves.

As mentioned earlier, tape recorder became a successful tool to gather women at one place, as they were very much fond of listening their voices recorded on tape (photo-l). Several women meetings were held and different participatory methods of data collection were applied. The 'handing over the stick' to these women proved a great response and they began recognising their innate ability to share their ideas through maps and diagrammes despite being illiterate. It was the time when they demanded to initiate a functional literacy programmes in three villages. On their extensive demand of being literate the researcher started a functional litteracy programme by forming interested women groups in three villages. One slate, one book (alphabetical) and chalks were distributed to each woman in the group. The programme was later supplemented with different awareness generation sessions. Consequently,

Table 1: Caste-wise Distribution of the Villages

	Villages													
	Nunwat		Aurawantand		Musahar		Shahpur		Semar		Karmaband		Total	
	No.*	%age*	No.	%age	No.	%age	No.	%age	No.	%age	No.	%age	No.	%age
Khawar	62	(78.48)	18	(69.24)	-	-	50	(75.75)	32	(65.30)	30	(50.00)	192	63.36)
Chamar	6	(7.60)	4	(15.39)	-	-	6	(9.09)	-	-	8	(13.33)	24	43.56)
Yadav	5	(6.33)	1	(3.84)	-	-	2	(3.04)	12	(24.48)	7	(11.66)	27	(8.91)
Musahar	1	(1.26)	-	-	23	(100)	-	-	3	(6.12)	-	-	27	(8.91)
Baniya	2	(2.33)	-	-	-	-	8	(12.12)	2	(4.08)	-	-	12	(3.96)
Brahman	3	(3.80)	-	-	-	-	-	-	-	-	-	-	3	(0.99)
Muslims	-	-	3	(11.54)	-	-	-	-	-	-	-	-	3	(0.99)
Chauhan	-	-	-	-	-	-	-	-	-	-	15	(25.00)	15	(4.95)
Total	**79**	**(100)**	**26**	**(100)**	**23**	**(100)**	**66**	**(100)**	**49**	**(100)**	**60**	**(100)**	**303**	**(100)**

* No. of families counted

** Figures in paranthesis show percentage of the total population of the respective villages.

*** Caste refers to the class or district hereditary order of society.

Table - 1 Shows the village-wise caste group distribution of responsdent in Naugarh block. It may be clearly noticed from the table that majority (63%) of respondents belong to Kharwar caste *(SC* Category); Brahmins and Muslims were found to be in marginal percentage (0.99%)

The respondents as depicted in the subsequent tables comprise of entire women population in the study area :

Table 2: (Distribution of respondents according to their age group)

Age**	Villages													
	Nunwat		Aurawantand		Musahar		Shahpur		Semar		Karmaband		Total	
(Years)	No.	%age*	No.	%age	No.	%age	No.	%age	No.	%age	No.	%age	No.	%age
20-40	56	(72.88)	14	(53.85)	9	(39.14)	30	(45.46)	30	(61.23)	24	(39.99)	163	(43.56)
40-60	23	(29.12)	10	(38.46)	14	(60.86)	33	(50.88)	18	(36.73)	34	(56.67)	132	(43.56)
>60	-	-	2	(7.69)	-	-	3	(4.64)	1	(2.04)	2	(3.34)	8	(2.64)
Total	**79**	**(100)**	**26**	**(100)**	**23**	**(100)**	**66**	**(100)**	**49**	**(100)**	**60**	**(100)**	**303**	**(100)**

* Figures in parenthesis shows percentage.
** Age refers to the number of full years completed at time of investigation.
Table - 2 dispicts that maximum women belonged to 20-40 years age group where as senior citizens are rarely found.

Table 3: Distribution of respondents and their literacy status

Literacy Status**	Villages													
	Nunwat		Aurawantand		Musahar		Shahpur		Semar		Karmaband		Total	
	No.	%age*	No.	%age	No.	%age	No.	%age	No.	%age	No.	%age	No.	%age
Illiterate	75	(94.94)	24	(92.31)	23	(100)	65	(98.48)	49	(100)	58	(96.67)	294	(97.02)
Literate	4	(5.06)	2	(7.69)	-	-	1	(1.52)	-	-	2	(3.33)	9	(2.98)
Total	**79**	**(100)**	**26**	**(100)**	**23**	**(100)**	**66**	**(100)**	**49**	**(100)**	**60**	**(100)**	**303**	**(100)**

*Figures in parenthesis shows percentage

** It refers to the ability of respondents to read and write with understanding.

Table 4: (Distribution of respondents according to their age group)

Income** (Rs.)	Villages													
	Nunwat		*Aurawantand*		*Musahar*		*Shahpur*		*Semar*		*Karmaband*		*Total*	
	No.	*%age**	*No.*	*%age*	*No.*	*%age*	*No.*	*%age*	*No.*	*%age*	*No.*	*%age*	*No.*	*%age*
10000	7	(8.86)	1	(3.84)	23	(100)	13	(19.69)	16	(2.04)	24	(39.99)	84	(27.72)
10000-60000	70	(88.60)	24	(92.32)	-	-	53	(80.31)	33	(97.96)	34	(56.67)	214	(92.42)
>60000	2	(2.54)	1	(3.84)	-	-	-	-	-	-	2	(3.34)	5	(1.66)
Total	**79**	**(100)**	**26**	**(100)**	**23**	**(100)**	**66**	**(100)**	**49**	**(100)**	**60**	**(100)**	**303**	**(100)**

* Figure shows in parenthesis shows percentage.

** It refers to the gross money generated by the family through all means (Agriculture, wage earning, forest product collection, animal husbandry etc.).

Table 5: Classification of Families according to their land holdings.

Land (Bigha)	Villages													
	Nunwat		*Aurawantand*		*Musahar*		*Shahpur*		*Semar*		*Karmaband*		*Total*	
	No.	*%age**	*No.*	*%age*	*No.*	*%age*	*No.*	*%age*	*No.*	*%age*	*No.*	*%age*	*No.*	*%age*
No Land	-	-	-	-	21	(91.31)	-	-	-	-	-	-	21	(6.94)
>2	23	(29.12)	7	(26.92)	2	(8.69)	58	(87.87)	28	(57.15)	32	(53.33\4)	150	(49.50)
2-4	52	(65.82)	13	(50.00)	-	-	8	(12.13)	16	(32.65)	23	(38.33)	112	(36.96)
>4	4	(5.06)	6	(23.08	-	-	-	-	5	(10.20)	5	(8.33)	20	(6.60)
Total	**79**	**(100)**	**26**	**(100)**	**23**	**(100)**	**66**	**(100)**	**49**	**(100)**	**60**	**(100)**	**303**	**(100)**

* Figure in parenthesis shows percentage

** Land holding refers to the possession of land which they use for agriculture or other purposes.

Table 4 Clearly shows the average annual income of respondents.

Maximum (90.42 per cent) families have the annual income of ₹ 10,000 ₹ 60,000. About (27.72 per cent) families were found having an average annual income of less than ₹ 10,000 which means that they struggle a lot to meet their basic requirements.

Regarding economic life of these people, they have forest-based economy. The sources of income in the locality is limited to (1) Agriculture, (2) Forest, (3) Livestock and (4) Manual Labour. These are the confined sources of income through which an average family consisting of three adults and three children earn to meet their subsistence.

The lands for farming is devoid of irrigation facilities and generally yield one single annual crop, which hardly meets their subsistence. Thus, they are dependent on forest for their livelihood. Livestocks are not productive and are only reared for cash income in crisis periods. Manual work in the deptt. of irrigations, deptt. of forest and migration in nearby cities add some cash income to their economy. Migration is however limited to the male members only, but in all other earning avenues, women equally participate in the family. She is backbone of a family as she has the responsibility of household work as well as outside work.

It was found that almost all families of these villages take loan to balance the deficit maximum amount of taking loan is up to ₹ 3000 to 4000. Mahajans gives the loan at the higher interest rate. In case of taking loan as kind, which is generally taken in the crisis of food grains (Quar Kartik) is repaid in double quantity in harvesting or forest product collection seasons. These mahajans avoid to take payment in cash due to less profit in the same. Heavy loan is taken in marriages, death or sickness. There was hardly any family who was out of the grip of indebtedness. Their whole life spend only in fulfilling their basic requirements of food, shelter and clothing.

From Table 5, it may concluded that majority (49.50 per cent) of families were having less than 2 bighas of land. However, every villagers do have small gram sabha (as) land (area of 1-2 bighas) after capturing the forest land area.

Regarding the types of houses in the villages it was found that in almost all villages, *Kachcha* houses were build up. There was rarely any *pakka* house in the villages. It was operationalised as material used for the construction of house.

As per family type, nuclear family system was prevailing in the area. Nuclear family was operationalised as composition of members of only person and includes minors and children only.

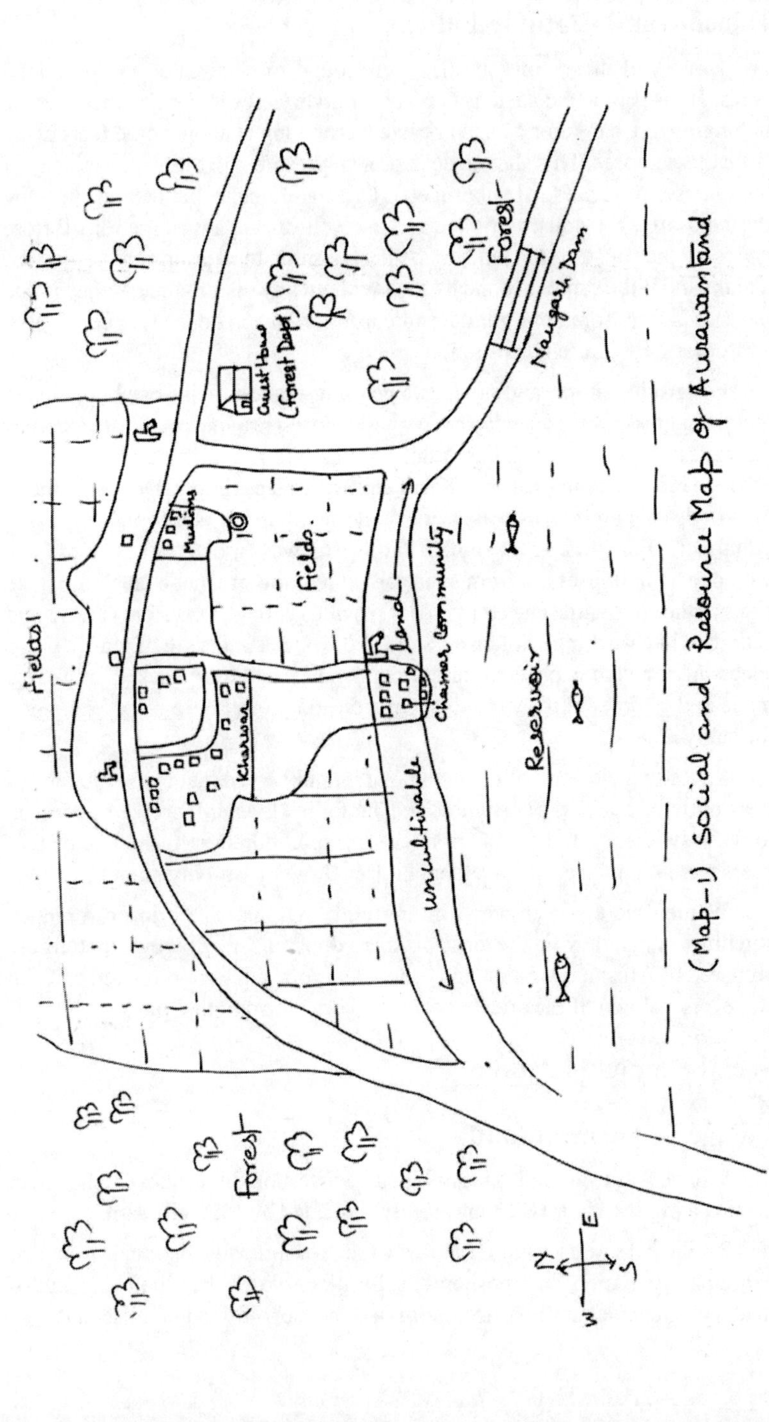

(Map-1) Social and Resource Map of Aurawantand

Housing and Clothing Pattern

Houses of these communities were found to be situated in the upland areas. Houses of same caste group are built very close to each other. People belonging to Chamar or Musahar caste were living at about some feets away from these houses. This shows the casticism prevalent in the area. Majority of their houses were made of unburnt clay. One traditional belief behind choosing the land area for construction was observed during investigation. Before choosing the construction land area, they put some food grains on the land for a night and if the same is found as such without any disturbance, it meant that the area is free from devils and termite infestation and hence was considered appropriate for house construction.

For making simple and small cottages, forest products like bamboo, timber, thatching grass, fibres and clay are required. Forest provides all these materials free of cost. Some of the important species like Asna, Kadamb, Shisham, Sakhu, Gurch, Kumbi, Karaya, Kikar etc. are used as timber. Doors are made of woods or bamboo. Roofs were made of khaprail, shrubs and grasses (Churwat). For binding of roof material, Banwar (a creeper) is used. The entrance of all houses are from courtyard and rooms are made on all the three sides of the courtyard. The courtyard is spacious enough to perform household activities like washing of utensils, storage of water, sundrying of grains. Open space in varandah is utilised for cooking and serving purposes. Chulha was made in the corner of the varandah. Only one door in a house was observed in the study area.

Regarding clothing of the women, it was observed that synthetic fabrics were prefered due to it's cheapness and durability. Even infants were observed to wear synthetic clothes. In summer season, children upto the age of five years were seen naked while elder children (boys) wear only gamcha.

Women were not engaged in any craft making. They do not practice stitching, rather, they tie the torn portion of dhoti or sari. However, pattals are prepared by Musahar women and broom and rope bags are prepared by each and every women of the area but for their own consumption only.

Social Economic Profile-

Village 1 (Aurawantand)

Village Aurawantand is surrounded by forest on three sides, in the south there is a big reservoir (Karmnasa river) bounded by Naugarh dam.

Social and resource map (Map-I), which was prepared by local women in participatory session, clearly shows the locations within the village in tenus of road, river, characteristics and condition of households and landuse patterns.

Village consisted of 26 families. Caste-wise distribution of family was as follows.

Caste	*No. of Families*	*Percentage*
Kharwar	18	69.1
Chamar	4	15.3
Yadav	1	3.8
Muslims	3	11.5
Total	**26**	**100**

Caste-wise separate living hamlets can be easily observed through the map, where Chamar and Muslim community reside 'away from the Kharwar community. A 'Kharanja' road interlinks the village to Naurgarh market. Only 30 per cent men and a lone woman were found literate upto the 8th standard. There is only one primary school in the village run by a NOO, (NCDC). Children have to go to Naugarh for further studies. Average size of the family was of 4-7 members. However, Muslim families consisted of 8-10 members.

Average land holding of the village was found to be 2-4 bighas per family. According to the women perception, there were three hand pumps and a welt in the village. Three families were having diesel pumps and only two families possessed a thresher.

Further analysis of socio-economic condition of women indicated that 40 per cent of their income was supported by the forest, 40 per cent from the agriculture and rest 20 per cent was supplemented through animal hubandry and labour work of forest irrigation departments.

As shown in the social map, low lands near to the reservoir could be easily irrigated through the reservoir, but the upland area was found to be unirrigated due to non-provision of irrigation channels. Due to this reason, they were dependent on the rain-water for their cultivations.

Animal population of the village (excluding those of Yadavs) consisted of 129 cows, 25 buffaloes, 20 goats and 40 bullocks. One Yadav family engaged in milk and milk product business was having 100 cows, 9 buffaloes, 26 goats and 4 bullocks.

Transact Analysis

A transact walk is participatory systematic walk for verification of various agro-ecological area mapped with informal discussions. This comes across on observation in the village during walk. The transect of the Aurawantand village is described as under (Map. 2).

Soil of the village is sandy loam. Microsituation of cultivated land is not conducive to agriculture production as the area is mostly rainfed. Paddy is

	Hillox	***Forest***	***Low Land***	***Village***	***Upland***	***Reservior***
Soil	Soil-Stone	Stone and Red	Loam	Sandy Loam	Sandy Loam	-
Crops and	-	-	Paddy	Wheat, Gram, Til,	Chilli, Brinsal, Beans etc.	Fishes
				Paddy, Maize etc.		
Natural Resource	Tendu, Piyar, Sakhu, Palash,	Forest, Trees	Forest, Trees	-	Forest, Trees	-
	Bel, Ber, Makoy etc.					
Live Stock	Grazing	Grazing	-	Cow, Goat, Buffaloe	Cow, Goat, Buffaloe etc.	Drinking
Problems	Erosion, Deforestation,	Erosion	Irrigation Problem	Education, Shortage of Safe drinking water,	Soil Erosion	-
	Lack of Fuel wood			Lack of Health facility,		
				Poor economic condition		

Map -2 Transect of Aurawantand.

grown in low land area where as maize and legumes are grown in upland situation. In rabi season, crops like mustard, gram, lentil etc are taken by the farmers. Forest provide tendu patta, piyar (chiraungi) seeds and mahua fruits which contribute a major part of their income. Villagers do have domestic animals like cows and goats but they are not for milking purpose as they are unproductive. They sell it in the market in crisis period for cash income. These animals graze in the forest and severely suffer from hunger in summer due to scarcity of grenary in the forest. Due to gradual deforestation, women have to walk long distances for fuel wood collection. Close proximity to the forest also creates problems of wild animals (like bears) attacks as they damage their crops during the seasons. They have to watch their fields day and night to save their crops from wild animals. When their husbands migrate to the nearby villages for labour, women were seen to guard their fields in the night also. Due to this, women have to share double work burden; during the day and in the night also. Mobility map shows the pattern of spatial mobility for women with respect to different activities (Map 3).

Women mobility map of Aurawantant village depicts that such mobility takes place on account of different reasons like health, visiting, shopping, collection of fuel, fodder and forest products, agricultural work etc. The women usually walk longer distances on foot on the rocky and Kharanja roads for the purpose. The map shows that they have relations in Bihar which also indirectly affects the culture of village. It is to be noticed here that due to degradation of forest, women have to walk long distances for fuel wood and forest product collection. For health problems also, they have to walk very long and hence sometimes, they ignore their sickness resulting in less work efficiency and ill health.

Socio-economic Profile of Village -2 (Nunwat)

Village Nunwat is connected with Naugarh market with rocky road which is 8 Km. away from the village. Village is surrounded by forest.

The dominant caste of the village is Kharwar. Castewise distribution of the village is as follows

S.No.	*Caste*	*No. of Families*	*Percentage*
1.	Kharwar	62	78.48
2.	Chamar	6	7.60
3.	Yadav	5	6.33
4.	Musahar	1	1.26
5.	Baniya	2	2.53
6.	Brahman	3	3.80
	Total	**79**	**100**

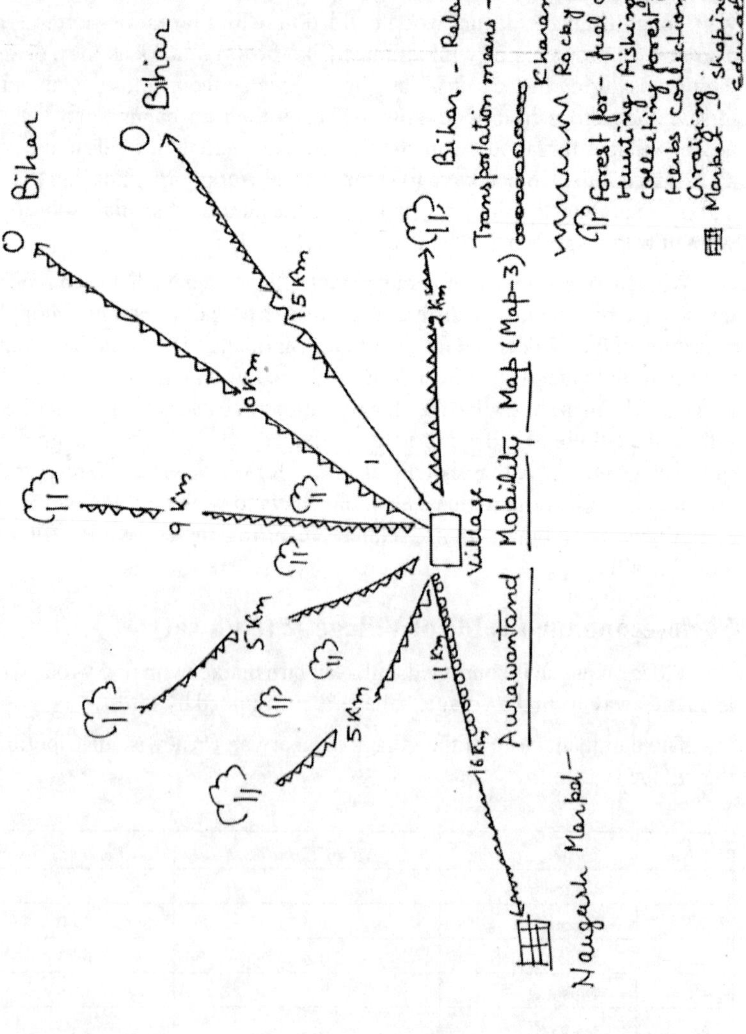
Bihar
Bihar
15 Km
10 Km
9 Km
5 Km
5 Km
11 Km
16 Km
2 Km
Village
Naugarh Market-
Aurawantand Mobility Map (Map-3)
Bihar - Relation
Transportation means - Bycycle and Barefoot
Kharanja Road
Rocky Road.
Forest for - fuel collection
Hunting, Fishing
collecting forest food products
Herbs collection
Grazing
Market - shoping, health,

Only one primary school and an anganwadi centre was found in the village. But, both institutions were functioning marginally. Researcher tried to visit the block pramukh (woman) residing in the village but she didn't come out from her house as she was afraid of any enquiry against...her. Villages also complained about her inactiveness and disinterest towards village welfare.

The village has four hand pumps and a well. Women in the area used to take bath in open on hand pumps and most of them also clean their utensils on handpump. They use to wash their clothes on pokhar away from the village. This took more time and energy and thus sometimes, they were bound to wear dirty clothes regularly even for a week. Women generally feel uncomfortable to take bath satisfactorily due to presence of men-folk on handpumps or their tendency to roam about near the area.

The average land holding was two to four bighas per head. The village does not possess any source of irrigation except rain. As shown in the social and resource map (Map 4), due to close vicinity to forest area, their crops are more succeptible to damage due to wild animal infiltration.

The women in the area are subjected to early marriages and early child bearing. First pregnancy was observed before attaining the 18 years of age. The average age of marriage among women is 13 years in contrast to 15 years in men. The average size of family comprised of 4-7 members. Nuclear family system is prevalent in the area.

As far as literacy status of women is concerned, 98 per cent of them were found illiterate. However, they are slowly recognising the importance of education and have started sending their daughters to schools for primary education.

Main source of their livelihood is agriculture alongwith forest products collection, animal husbandary and labour work. Seven men (8 per cent) were found engaged in occupations like drivery, carpentery, khoa making, pattal making and shopkeeping. As per animal population in the village, there were 177 cows, 43 buffaloes, 316 goats and 75 bullocks. These animals are mostly unproductive and supplement villager's income by selling it in crisis period. (Map. 5 and 6) which were prepared by local women show the transact analysis and mobility.

Socio-economic Profile of Village -3 (Musahar)

Musahar village is situated about half a km away from the Nunwat village. All inhabitants of the village belong to Musahar caste. This caste is identified as Mush (Rat) catcher and consumer. They are migrants from the state of Bihar and are considered as untouchables in the area.

They are 26 (twenty six) nuclear families in the area. An average family consist of three adults and four children. All Kachcha houses were seen there.

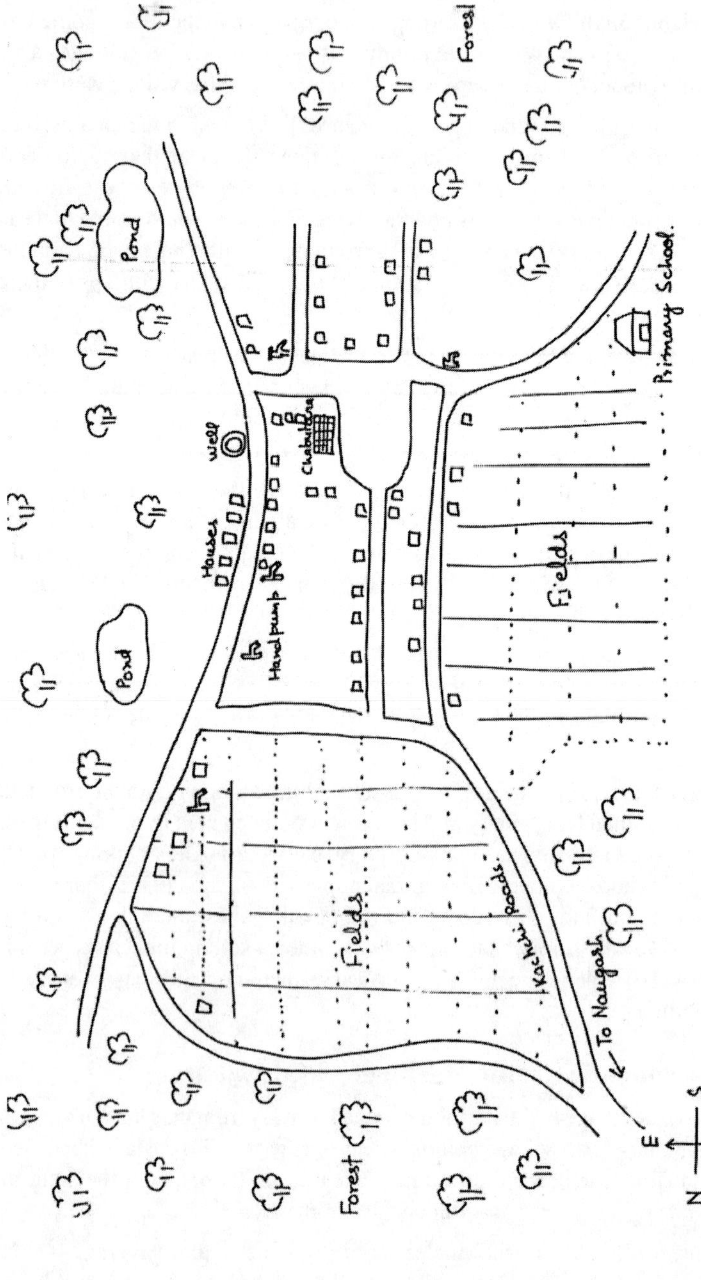

(Map-4) Social and Resource Map (Nunwat)

Land Type	***Hillox***	***Forest Land***	***Village***	***Low Land***	***Upland***	***Mushar Village***	***Upland***	***Forest***
Soil	Stone	Sandy loam	Red. Sandy loam	Laom	Sandy loam	Sandy loam	Red. Sandy loam	Sandy loam
Crops	-	-	Wheat, Mustard,	Paddy	Wheat, Mustard, Maize,	Potato, Brinjal,	Wheat, Gram,	-
			Gram, Pea, Linud		Pea, Mustard, Linseed	Pea Lentil, Pea	Pea, Lentil	Mahua, Tendu, Piyar, Ber,
Trees	Mahua, Piyar, Tendu,	Sagaun, Palash, Bel, Ber,	Banana, Papaya, Guavava,	Mahua, Gular	Mahua, Harre, Bahera,	Pipal, Mahua, Imli,	Jamun, Pipal, Mahua	Sagaun, Karkonda etc.
	Karonda, Ber, Aaunla etc.	Mahua, Piyar, Tendu etc.	Banbu, Babul etc.		Gular, Piyar etc.	Gular, Bambu		
Problems	Soil Erosion	Erosion, Forest, Degradation	Poor economic condition,	Erosion and Irrigation	Erosion	Poor economic condition,	Erosion and Irrigation	Degradation of forest
			Lack of Irrigation facilies,			Lack of Irrigation facilies,		over grazing
			Wild Animal Infliction					

Transect Map of Nunwat and Musahar -(Map -5)

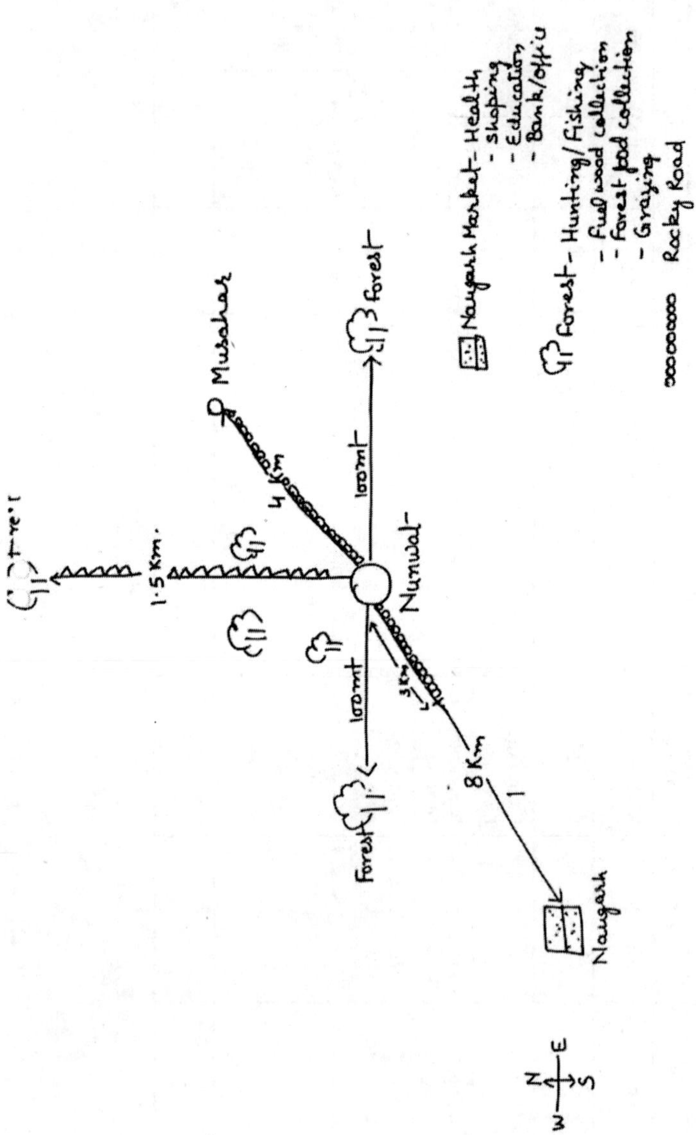

Mobility Map of Women in Nunwat (Map-6)

Some Pakka houses were built under the scheme of Indira AwasYojana but all of them are not in living conditions.

As shown in the 'social and resource map (Map 7), the village is very near to the forest (i.e. only 50 mt. away). One well and a handpump was found as the source of water but the well was not functional. The link road to the village Nunwat gets water logged in the rainy season. Pokhar (Pond) is generally used for bathing and fishing purposes.

Total land holding of the village was found at 15-20 Kattha only. As can be studied from the table, the family-wise distribution of land holding is only marginal. Distribution of respondents according to their land holdings is only marginal.

Distribution of respondents according to their land holdings

S.No.	*Land Holidng (Bigha)*	*Families*
1.	No Land	21
2.	<2	2
3.	2-4	-
4.	>4	-
	Total	**23**

Main crops grown in the area are Tisi, Arhar, Chana, Masur. They could not grow paddy due to lack of proper irrigation facility. One family of the village was found having kitchen garden in their home. The responsibility to maintain the kitchen garden laid on women in the family. Vegetables as well as fruits were grown in the garden for their domestic consumption and also for sale.

The main occupation of the village includes making leaf plates, honey collection and agricultural labour (Photo No 2). Since they do not have much land area, they have to depend entirely on the forest. Total animal population of the village includes 2 cows, 1 buffalo, 4-5 goats and some hens.

Inhabitants of the village are economically downtrodden and are forced to depend on forest produce for food. Many-a-times, the forest produce does not suffice for their hunger, and hence they have to undergo the torture of starvation oftenly. Forest produce are often bartered for other food items.

The products are also sold for cash income. Men and women alike do the labour work in forest department, irrigation department and fields of nearby cities. There are migration to other cities for labour activities.

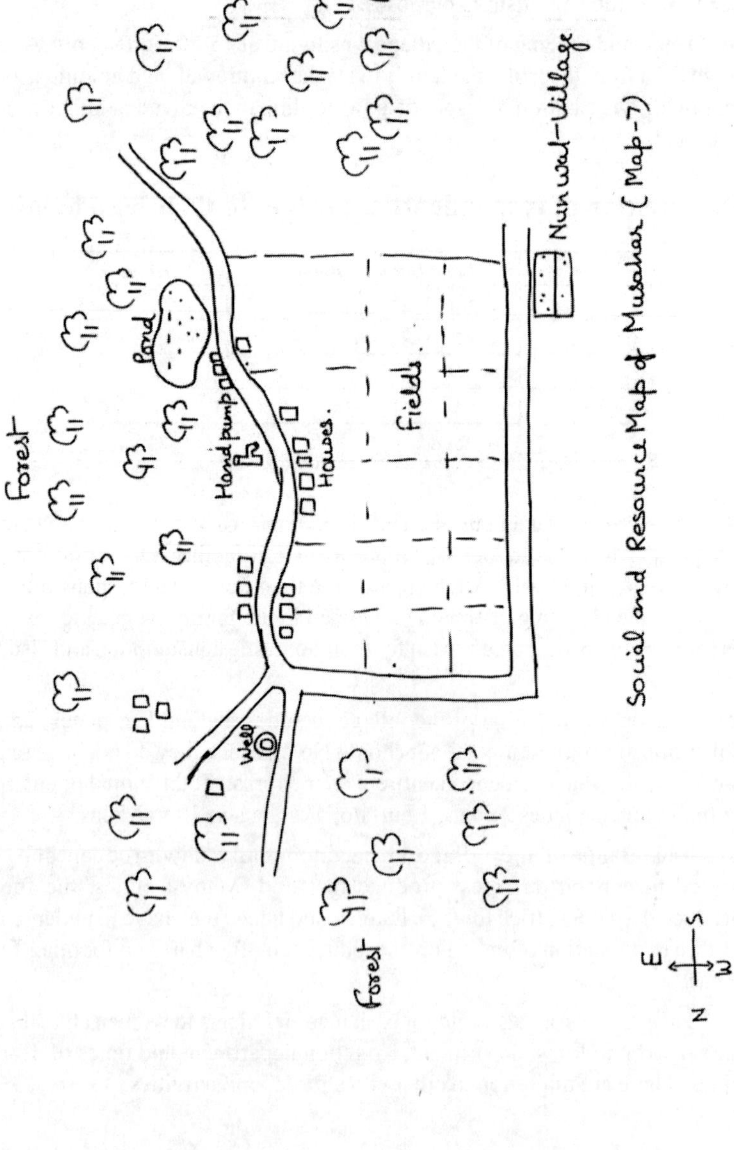

Social and Resource Map of Musahar (Map-7)

Photo—showing a women perparing leaf plates in Musahar Village.

Photo—showing women harvesting of wheat in Aurawantand village.

Seasonal work Calender (Month-wise) is shown as under

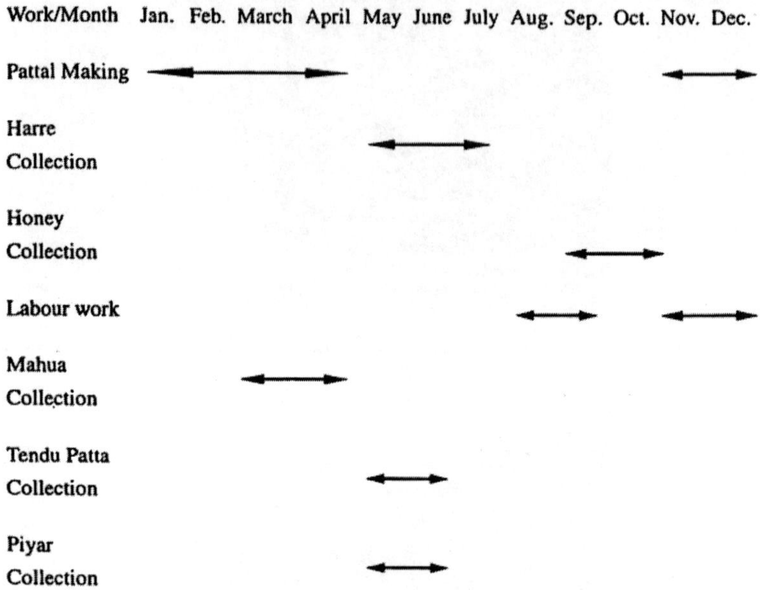

Seasonal work calender of Musahar Toli clearly indicates the distribution of work during various months of the year. From the table it may be concluded that works that require hard labour and time like Pattal making and collection of Harre, Mahua, Piyar and Tendu leaves mainly done by women. However, men also participate in the same, with little responsibility. Men migrate in nearby cities for labour work. Labour work includes, agricultural work, rikshaw pulling, labour work of forest and irrigation departments.

The literacy status of the village shows that all women were found illiterate in the area. When enquired about the same, they replied that they knew to write their names but now they have forgotten even that. Marriages at the tender age of 13 (girls) and 15 (boys) is done here.

Transact analysis as shown under the transact of Nunwat village (Map-5) reflects that they have small land holdings in which they grow wheat, maize, gram, pea and lentil.

Mobility map (Map-5) shows the movement of women in different direction for different purposes. Women go to forest for collecting fuel wood, leaves for pattal making, honey and forest fruits. For shopping and health problems, they have to go to Chakiya, Naugarh, Aurawantand and Madhopur, which are respectively 36 km., 9 km., 66 km. and 14 km away from their

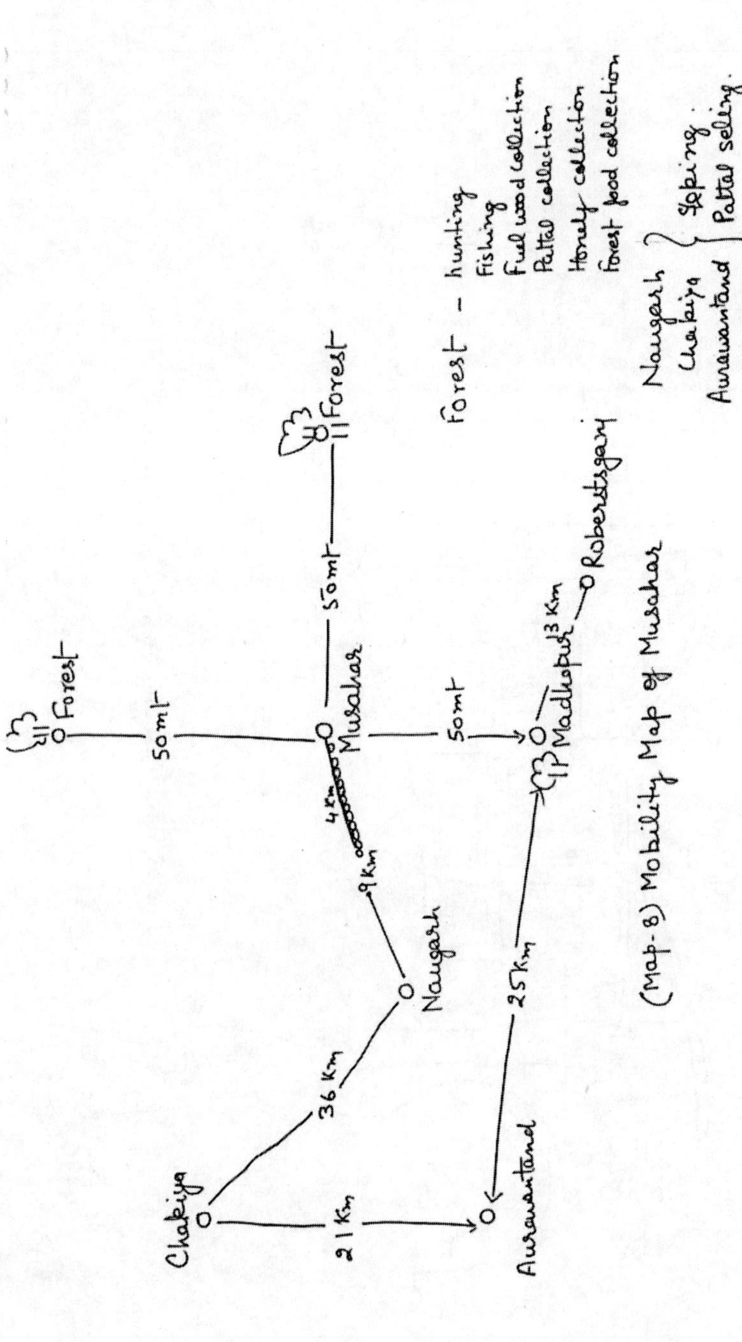

(Map-8) Mobility Map of Musahar

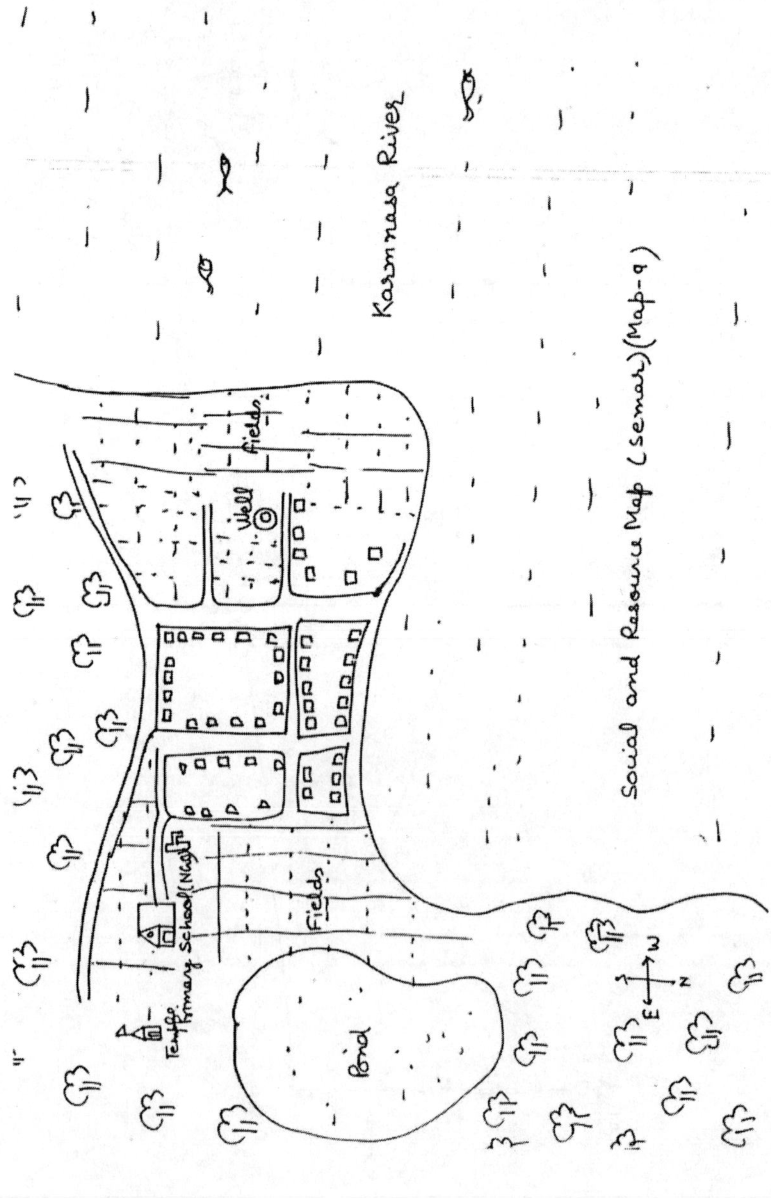
Karmnasa River
Fields
Well
Fields
Temple
Primary School (Night)
Pond
E
W
N
Social and Resource Map (Semar) (Map-9)

village. They have to walk on foot only on the rocky roads. Pattal selling is the business of men only.

A case study regarding their economy is described under the topic titled 'A Case Study of Musahar'.

Socio-economic Profile of Village - 4 (Semar)

Semar village is surrounded by forest from three sides. Bihar is about 9 km, away from the village. There is lack of proper link road to the village, therefore, one has to face much difficulty to meet the basic requirements like shopping and health facilities. They have to go to Chakiya for these purposes which is 53 km. away from the village. There is one primary school in the village. The village has one well and a handpump only. The well is never cleaned and women take bath and wash their clothes near the well in the open (Map 9).

S.No.	*Caste*	*Population*	
		*No.**	*%age*
1.	Kharwar	32	65.30
2.	Yadav	12	24.48
3.	Musahar	3	6.12
4.	Baniya	2	4.08
	Total	**49**	**100**

* No of families counted.

Pond adjoining the village is the source for washing clothes. The social and resource map of the village clearly shows that the village is surrounded on three sides by forest and one side by forest and one side by Karmnasa river. A major problem being faced by the villagers is the annual and almost regular flood during the rainy season (Photo-3).

They have limited source of income due to shortage of farm land holdings. Average land holding is 4-5 bigha per person. Like other villages, they are also dependent on forest for their subsistence. There are 15 Yadav families who are engaged in milk and milk product business in the village. Women were found to prepare Khoa (a milk product) in the home (Photo-4).

No woman was found literate in the village. However, one man and six children were found literate upto primary level.Yadav families engaged in milk and milk product business have 25 to 30 cows, others have an average of 4-6 cows in their house. Two families were having 25-30 goats. Total animal population of the village is as follows :

Photograph taken from Semar Village showing topographical location of the Village. Photo (3)

Karmnasa river, which is flooded during rainy season.

Women participating in Khoa making process.

A women carrying a bundle of avested wheat plantations agricultural field. Photo (4)

Animal	*No.*
Cows	268
Poultry	66
Goats	142
Buffaloes	66

Radio sets are the only means of information and entertainment in the village. The entire village had only two sets of radio. Women prefer to listen women related programmes, songs and news items.

Mobility map (Map-10) of Semar village shows the close vicinity to the forest area. Forest area is about 50 mt, 20 mt and 100 mt in the east, south and west direction of the village respectively. Thus, collection and sale of forest products can be add done conveniently and hence valuable income to their economy. The crops of paddy, mustard pea, linseed and vegetables are grown for their own consumption (transact Map 11). Surplus are rarely sold for cash income, as the production itself is very low.

Socio-economic Profile of Village - 5 (Karmabandh)

This village is situated about 3 km away from Naugarh market and is properly linked by road. Thus, this village is somewhat in a better condition than others. The village has got in total 60 nuclear families. Caste wise distribution is as follows :

S.No.	*Caste*	*Population*	
		No.	*%age*
1.	Chauhan	15	25.00
2.	Kharwar	30	50.00
3.	Yadav	7	11.66
4.	Chamar	8	13.33
	Total	**60**	**100**

Women in the area prepared the social and resource map which indicates that there were two handpumps and a well are the only sources of drinking water (Photo 5) Well is never chlorinated and thus unhygienic for drinking and cooking purposes. The village is closely surrounded by forest on three sides (Map-12). Women complained about damaging of their crops due to intrusion of forest animals. There are two primary schools in the village. Main occupation of the village includes fanning, brick-making, collection of tendu, piyar and mahua. Crops of paddy, wheat, pea, mustard, potato and lentil are grown in the village (Map-13).

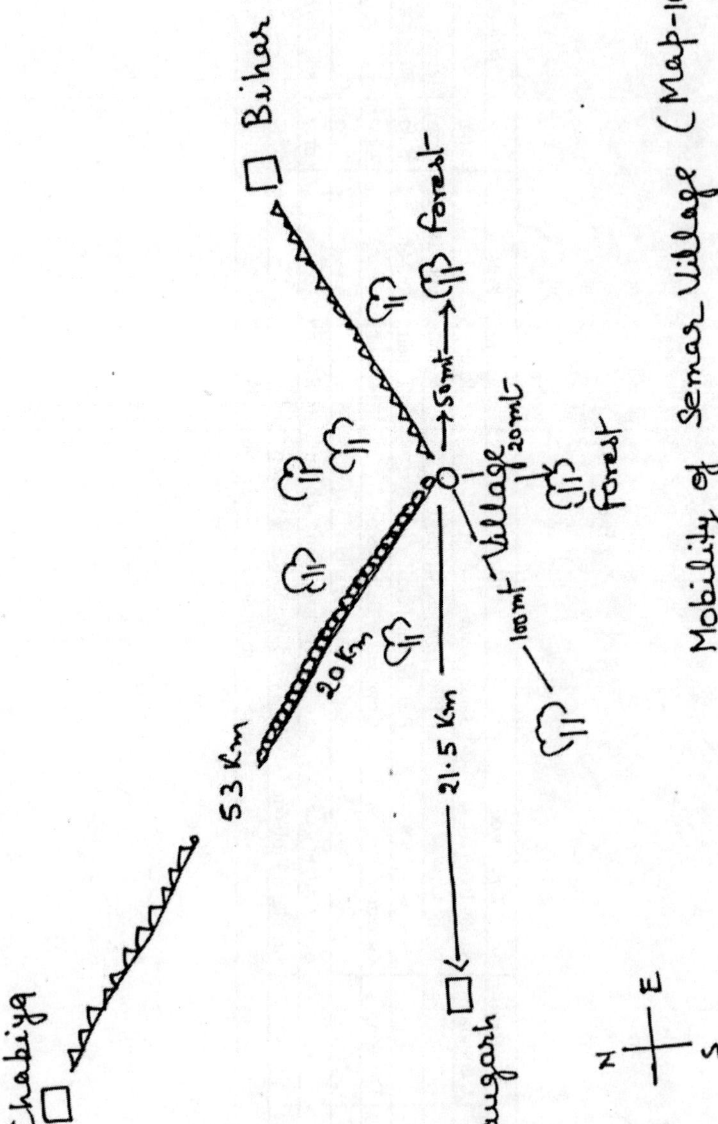

Mobility of Semar Village (Map-10)

Land Type	***Reservior***	***Low Land***	***Village***	***Forest***	***Hillox***
Soil	Clay loam	Sandy loam	Sandy loam	Red	Stone
Crops	-	Paddy	Chilli, Brinjal, Mustard,	Mahua, Piyar, Sakhu,	Piyar, Mahua,
			Pea, Linseed etc.	Tendu, Anola etc.	Sakhu, Palash, etc.
Live-Stock	Drinking	Grazing	Cow, Goat, Bullocks,	Grazing	Grazing
			Calues, Poultry etc.		
Problems	-	Sedimentation and	Education, Irrigation Problem	Erosion	Erosion and Deforestation
		Irrigation Problem	and Flooding in Rainy Season		

Transect Map of Semar Village (Map- 11)

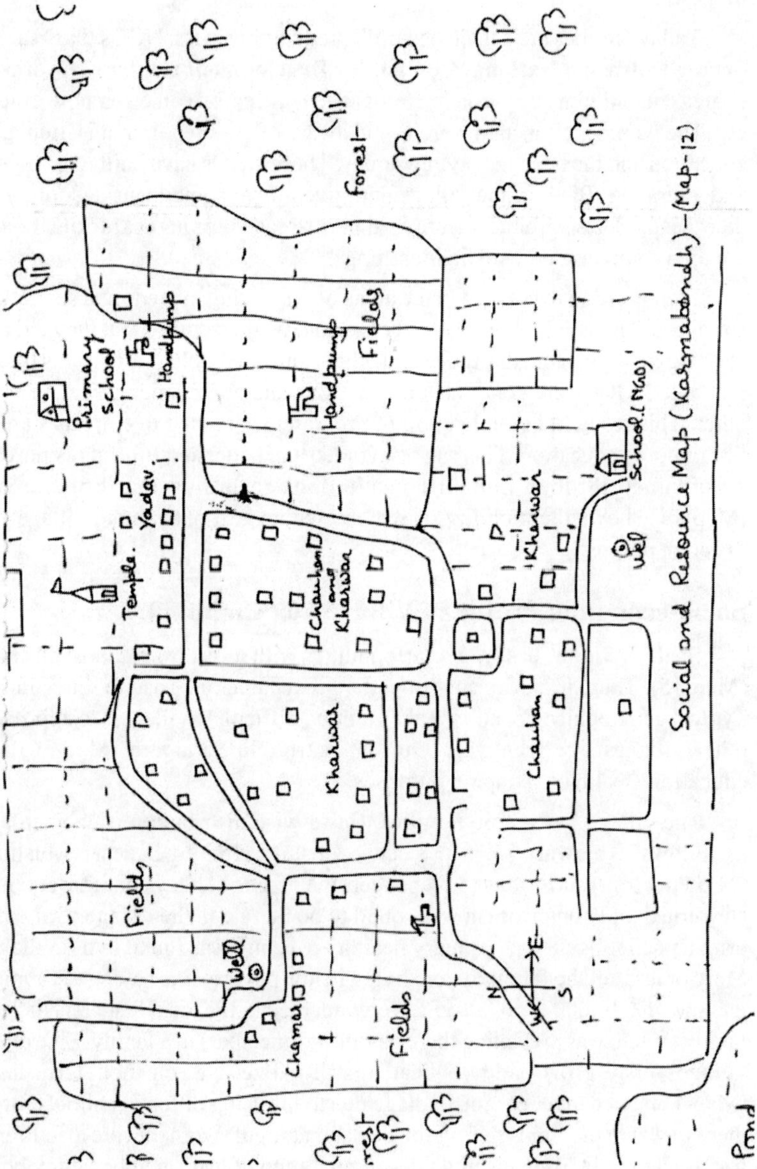
Primary school
Handpump
Temple
Yadav
Forest
Fields
Handpump
Chauhan and Kharwar
Kharwar
Kharwar
Chauhan
School (NGO)
Well
Fields
Well
Chamar
Fields
N
E
W
S
Pond
Social and Resource Map (Karmabandh)—(Map-12)

Only one woman of the village was found to be literate. Girls upto the age of 15 years were found to be literate up to the primary level. Transact analysis like that of other villages shows the soil type, crops and vegetation and problems in the area.

Yadav families are engaged in milk products business. NGOs like **Manav Seva Kendra** and **National Council for Development Centre** are working in areas of children education, maternal and child care, women empowerment etc. The women in the area were found aware of children immunisation, girl education and the need for saving money. These NGOs have built up a Mahua and Chiraungi Bank in the village and given them some loans according to their needs. These products were sold in off-season for higher profits. Loans are then compensated with their earnings.

They were also working in the areas of improving hygiene and sanitation condition. The village was neat and clean and women opined that they did not eat stale foods to avoid diarrhoea and other stomach problem. But it was found that both NGOs were very much competitive and non-cooperative with each other. This resulted in duplication in programmes related to emphasis areas like children education. This can be avoided and better and fruitful results can be obtained through mutual consultations regarding the thrust areas. (Map-14) shows the mobility of women within and outside the village for different purposes.

Socio-economic Profile of Village - 6 (Shahpur)

Shahpur village has got its surroundings with forest from almost all sides (Map-15). There is hardly any proper approachable link road to this village. Typical geographical location makes it more difficult to villagers to approach other villages like Khaliyari, Oini Naugarh and Saraigarh (Map-16) for education, health or shopping purposes.

The village has got 66 families. Caste-wise distribution of women are as follows: Kharwar (75.75 per cent), Chamar (15.39 per cent), Muslims (11.54 per cent) and Yadav (3.84 per cent). As far as literacy among women is concerned, only one woman was found to be literate in the village. Only one primary school, but none primary healthcare centre was found in the Village. More or less, all the families were living below poverty line having the annual income of ₹ 10,000 ₹ 60,000 and were indebted to the local lenders. Nuclear family system was prevailing there having 4-7 members in a family. Like other villages, they grow paddy, wheat, lentil, maize. etc. on their farm land (Map-17), but danger of crop damage due to intrusion of forest animals force them to watch the fields during the day and at night. Women were also found watching their fields in the night due to migration of male members for labour work.

	Low Land	***Village***	***Village***	***Upland***	***Forest***
Soil	Sandy loam	Sandy loam	Sandy loam	Sandy loam	Stone
Land Use	Farm land	Village and Farm land	Village	Farm land and Grazing	Grazing and Forest Collection
Crops	Paddy	Wheat, Gram, Til,	Vegetables	Wheat and Vegetables	Forest trees
		Mustard, Potato			
Problems	Soil Erosion,	Lack of drinking	Lack of Irrigation	Lack of Improved	Deforestation Intrusion
	Irrigation Problem	and Irrigation water	water, Casteusm	Seedo, Fertilizers	of Wild Animals

(Map-13) Transect Map of (Karmabandh)

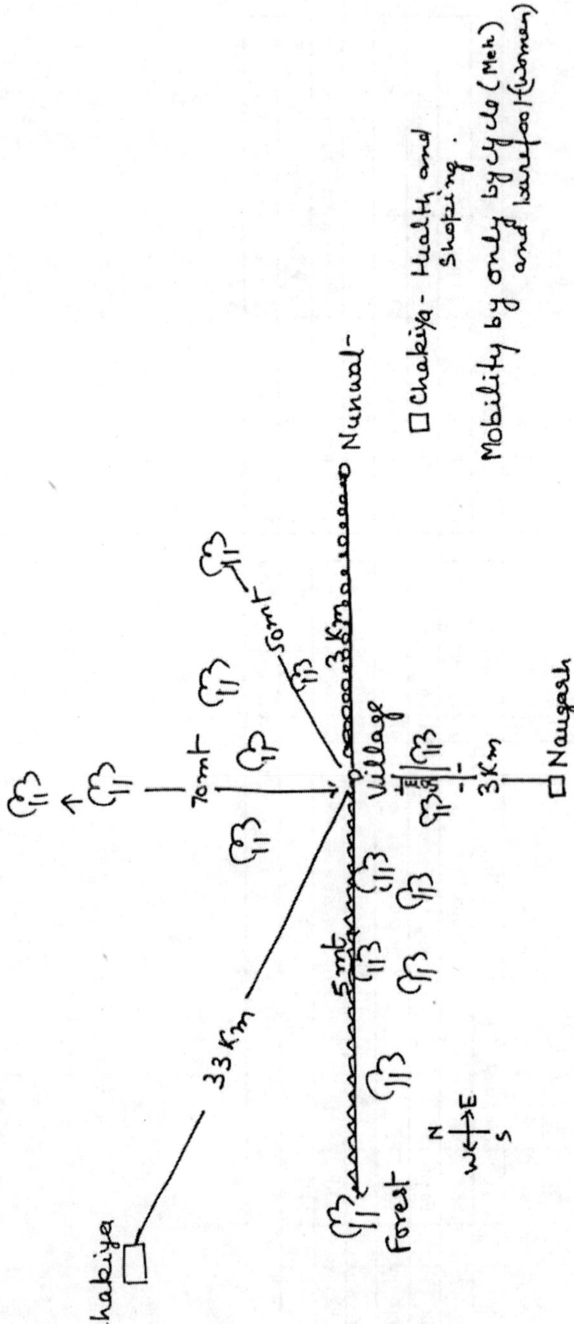

Mobility Map (Karmabandh) (Map-14)

Women of Karmab handh Village Participating in making social and Resource of their Village (photo)

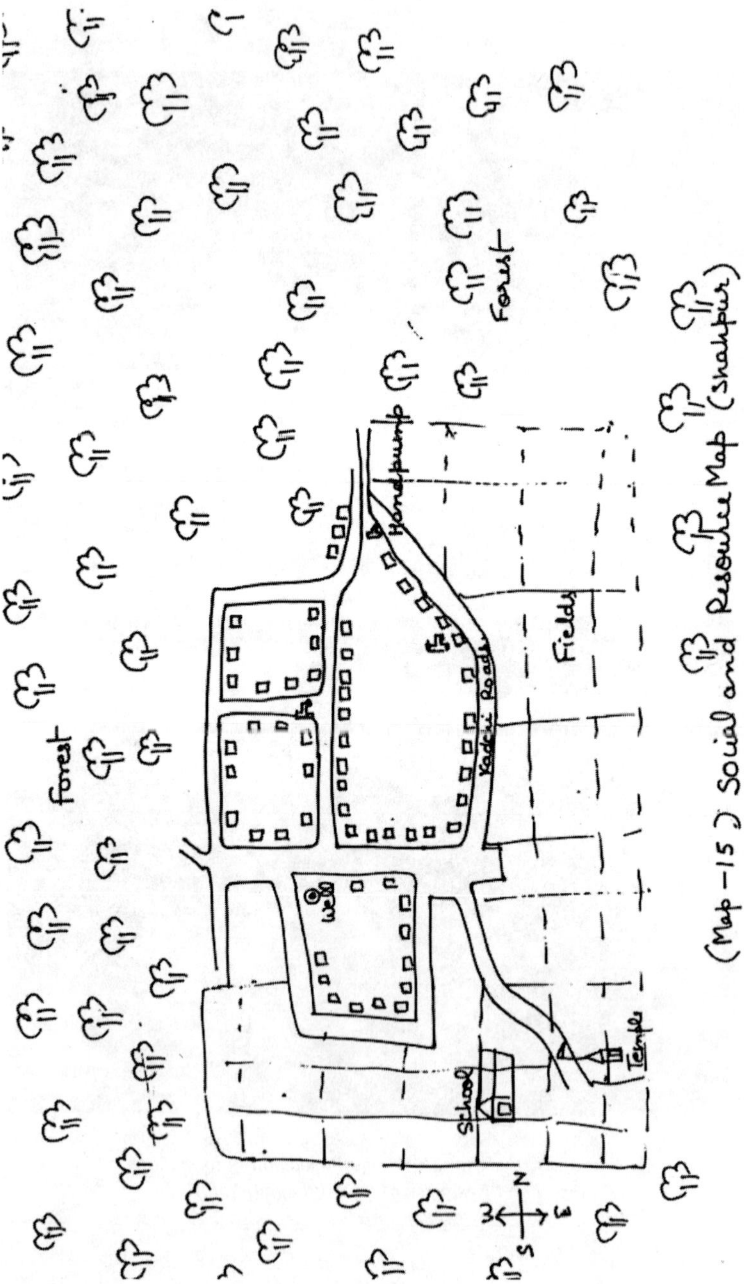

(Map-15) Social and Resource Map (Shahpur)

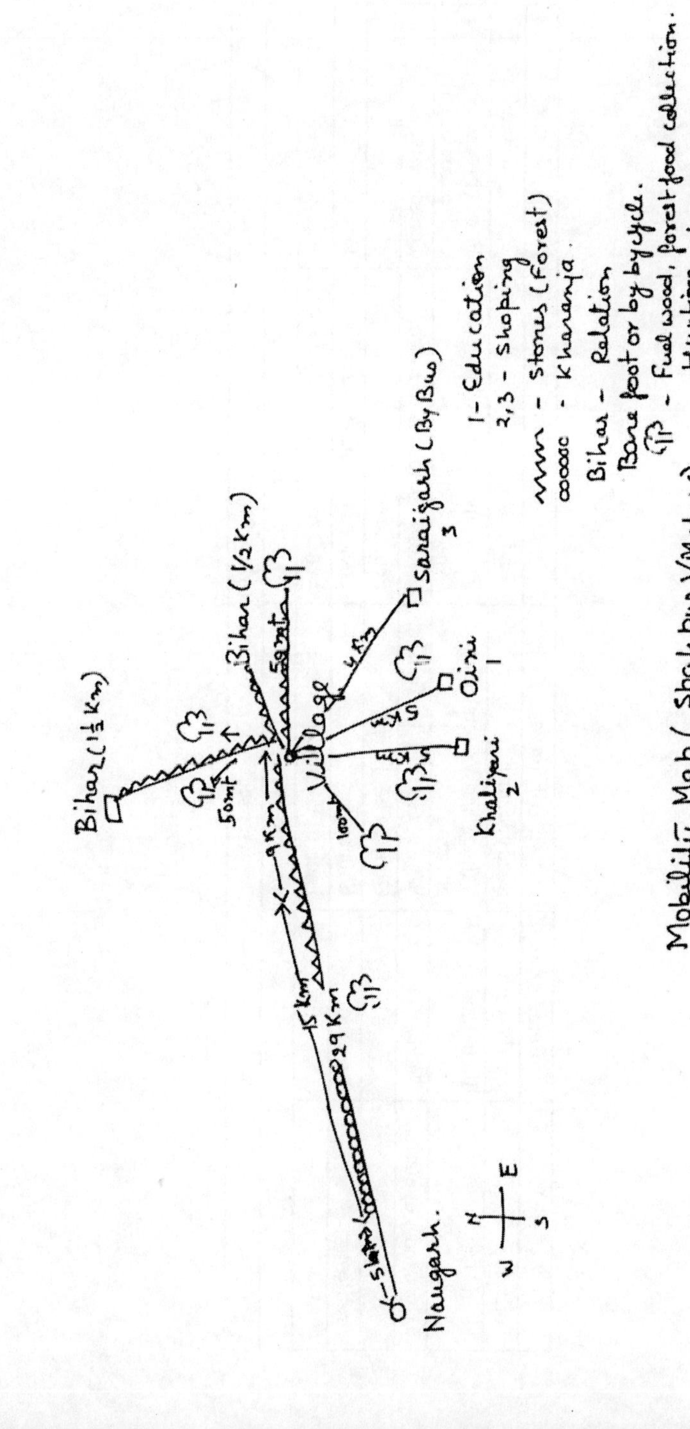
Bihar (1½ Km)
Bihar (1/2 Km)
Saraigarh (By Bus)
Village
Oini
Khaliyani
Naugarh.
N
S
E
W
1- Education
2,3 - Shoping
- Stones (Forest)
- Kharanja.
Bihar - Relation
Bare foot or by bycycle.
- Fuel wood, forest food collection.
Hunting etc.
Mobility Map (Shahpur)(Map-16)

	Low Land	***Village***	***Upland***	***Forest***
Soil	Sandy loam	Sandy loam	Sandy loam	Stone and Red Soil
Land Use	Farm land	Village and Vegetables growing	Farm land and Grazing	Forest product collection, Grazing
Crops and Vegetation	Paddy	Wheat, Gram, Til, Mustard,	Wheat, Gram, Til, Linseed,	Forest trees
		Gourd, Pea, Beans	Pea, Gram	
Problems	Irrigation	Education	Lack of Irrigation water,	Deforestation
		Lack of Health facilities,	Fertilizer and Improused seed,	
		Transportation problems	Animal Intrusion	

Transect map of Shahpur (Map- 17)

Livelihood Analysis

Livelihood analysis can be described by means of pie-diagram. It reveals the behaviour and adjustment strategies of farm families in different socio-economic situations. Individual family has its own way of living and means to pull on in different conditions for over a period of time.

Women of the all villages were having same Socio-economic status.

Livelihood source analysis as perceived by these women was analysed through a pie diagram, which shows that major source of income to sustain their livelihood was supported by agriculture and forest followed by animal husbandry and labour work elsewhere or in forest and irrigation departments.

During crisis, such as on the occasion of marriage, death, agricultural problems and sickness, they lend loans from local mahajans in form of mortgage of land, utensils or ornaments at 50 per cent to 60 per cent interest rate.

It was found that on the occasion of marriages, they borrow utensils, clothes and ornaments from the shopkeepers and bear loan burden of ₹ 10,000 to ₹ 12,000 and virtually live in debt trap throughout their lives. During the season of mahua and piyar production, villagers were seen to exchange it for rice, or vegetables. One kg of mahua was replaced by a kg of rice.

It was also found that women in the area do not save money for crisis period, i.e. the concept of saving was lacking. Reason behind the same was marginal income which barely met their day to day expenses.

Usually male members of the family migrate to nearby cities for labour work usually in the month of Feb. - April where they earn a paltry wage of Rs 40-50 a day.

Impact Analysis

The impact diagram clearly shows the unfavourable effects of environmental degradation on rural livelihood. In this method, the local people described cause-effect relationship, verbally and visually and explained linkages amongst different factors. Flow chart shows how, the factor like lack of availability of improved seeds, scarcity of irrigation water, lack of fertilisers and problem of wild animals are responsible for a crop failure and consequential impact ultimately result in increased hunger and starvation of people.

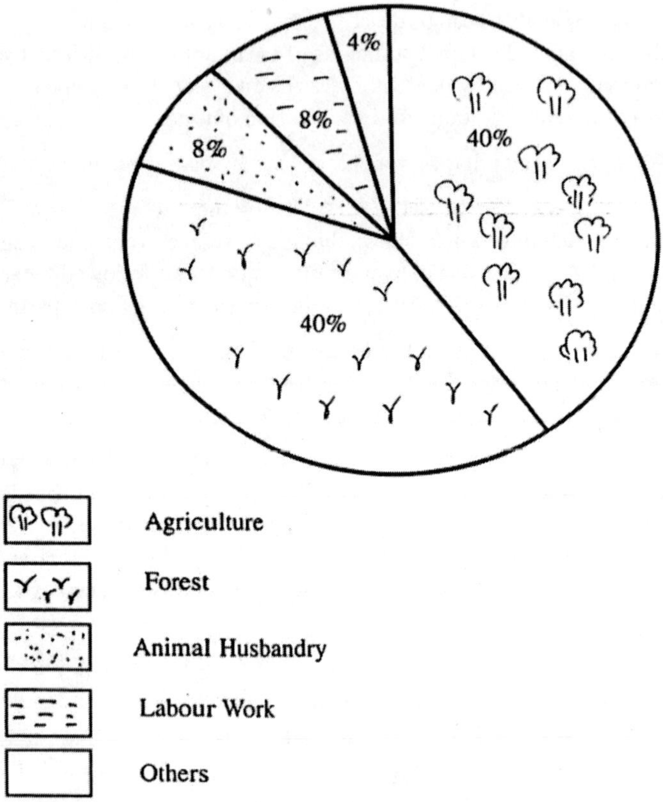

Crisis

- Marriage
- Death
- Agriculture
- Sickness

Cope With

- Mortgage of land utensils and ornaments
- loan from local mahajans at high interest

No concept of saving in the area

LIVELIHOOD ANALYSIS

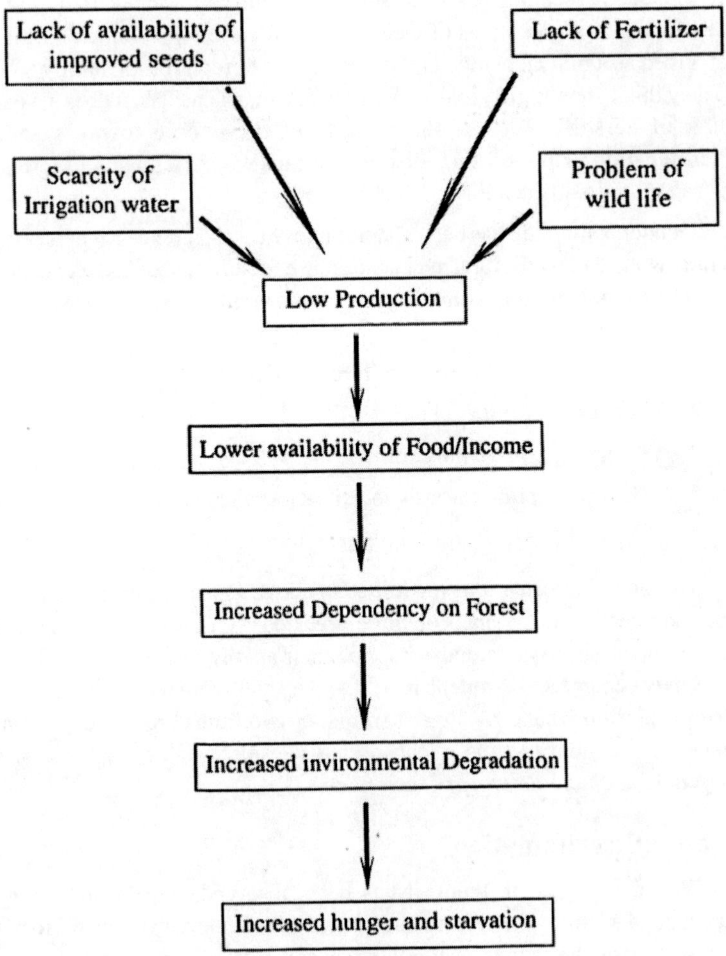

IMPACT ANALYSIS

OBJECTIVE - TWO

Gender Perception

Gender perception has been selected as an important variable which determines the social status of women in the area. How a women's entity is perceived as a human being? Is she treated as a burden for the family? What do they think about a girl child's education and marriage? What does a woman think of herself? What is the attitude of the people towards gender discrimination? How do they discriminate males and females in terms of education, food intake and work distribution?

Gender perception has been operationalised as differences in perceptions of rural women vis-à-vis rural men which make for differences in understanding and appreciation of rural issues. In this section, various gender related aspects have been covered up i.e. -

* Their daily routine or work force participation;
* Gender discrimination;
* Their decision-making ability;
* Their perception towards social issues; and
* Their attitude towards family planning.

To find the informations regarding all above aspects, various PRA tools were adopted. Rural women of these areas easily describe their opinions through open discussions; they describe their apathy towards life and some times they become sad about the harsh life they are living where the entire life goes in (Do Jun Khane Ka Jugad) arranging two times bread a day.Women also face secondary status in the society, despite performing almost all household and outdoor work of their homes.

Gender Discrimination

While staying with them, it has been observed that despite being a backbone of a family, they are not recognised as an important entity of society. Men still enjoy the primary status and feel superior of being a man.

Women in the area were never given the at par status in family and society. They feel that it is their responsibility to work according to men's desire. Still, they hold the decision-making power regarding some issues like, child marriage, education and purchasing household equipments.

The birth of a daughter is not considered good in the area. She gets an inferior status from women who have got a male child. Father only takes - interest in rearing up of male child. Male children are given preference in education, food and other needs. Women do not have rights related selling and purchasing of property including land, house or livestocks. Important decisions are taken by male persons with little or no consent from women in the family.

Inspite of all this, women perform almost all household and outdoor activities. She is involved in all agricultural activities except ploughing. Starting from sowing of seeds to harvesting of crops, she is engaged in all types of works. During sowing season of paddy or during harvesting, she spends upto ten hrs. a day in her farm continuously. Household activities like cooking, serving, washing clothes, cleaning utensils and home, fetching water, child care practices, livestock management, collecting fuel wood, collecting forest fruit products like mahua, tendu patta, piyar and makoy, making brooms, thapua for house building etc. are numerous activities in which she is involved with little recognition.

For understanding women's status in society, first, we have to look at the work performed by women. For this, daily routine work and seasona l work calendar has been prepared in open discussions with rural women (Photo-6).

Table 6: Daily Routine work of Women

Time	*Work*
5.30 Morning'	Wake up
6.00-7.00	Cleaning Animals, collecting compost.
7.00-9.00	Cleaning homes and water collection.
9.00-10.30	Kitchen arrangement, chulha making, preparation, serving and eating meals.
10.30-2.30	Seasonal work (field work, Thapua making, broom making, mudding etc
2.30-3.30	Taking bath, washing clothes, utensils, cleaning homes.
3.3.-5.3.0	Fuel collection, water collection.
6.00-7.00	Chulha making, food preparation, serving and eating foods.

Photo (6)

Threshing of graining done with the help of bulls by a village women.

Harvesting of paddy done by women.

Gender Discrimination as perceived by women

Researcher used to listen their folk songs for rapport building and to get closer to their lives. These songs were recorded and these women relistened their own voices with great interest. It became an important tool to collect various informations regarding different aspects.

Interestingly, some songs which were sung by these women in different villages in different ragas depicted the same story of discrimination against women and girl child. For example:

Folk Song

- **Kahe Karela More Babuji Dorangi Nitiya**
  (Why my father do dual policy)
- **Uhijan baba more, beta janaula se**
  Uhijan beti janamaula Hamre babuji
  (Father, from same parents, son has been born and daughter also)
- **Bhaiya ke padhave Khatir bhejla schooliya se**
  Hamre se ghar putaula hamre babuji,
  (You have send my brother for schooling and asked me to mud the home).
- **Bhaiya ke padhave Khatir deshva bideshva bhejala se**
  Hamre se bakari charaula Hamre babuji.
  (You have send my brother country or abroad for schooling and asked me to graze the goats).
  (by abroad they mean away from village)
- **Bhaiya ke khilave khatir khoya malai dihela**
  Hamre le dal bhat mohala hamre babuji
  (For feeding my brother, you have given him khoa and cream and for me rice and dal is only desired)
- **Bhaiya ke padhave khatir naukari dharai dihala**
  Hamre ke school nahi dikhaula Hamre babuji
  (For brother's education you have done labour work, but you even didn't sent me to school)
- **Bhaiya ke khabriya khatir jiyara taras gaila,**
  Dusare se chithiya bachaula hamre babuji.
  (For information regarding brother's well being, my heart gets thirsty. I have to give letters to others to read it out)
- **Bhaiya Ke Padhave Khatir rupaya paisa dihala,**
  Hamre se bartan manjaula hamre babuji.

(For borther's education, you give him money and asked me to clean kitchen utensils.

- **Mata hamari bali hamke samajhili ho,**
  Ek najar takali bhaiya bahini ko.
  (My mother understands me well and keep equal eyes to both of brother and sisters)
- **Nahi Det Gaiya Nahi det dahejava tu,**
  Panch tak school dekhaula hamre babuji

You neet not give me cow and dowry in my marriage but you must try to give us primary education.

Table 7: Seasonal work Calender (month-wise)

Month	Work
January	Sowing Rabi crops, guarding crops to save it from wild animals, gathering fuel-woods from forest, making Khaprail (Cupel) and baking it, making rope for bam boo cot and holding Khaprail, hunting from forest.
February	Guarding crops (day and night). Male migration for labour work in near by cities for 10-15 days.
March	Labour work, collecting mahua, making rope and khaprail, watching crops. Cutting & threshing of crops.
April	Collecting Mahua, cutting, threshing rice or other rabi crops, Labour work, making khaprail and houses.
May	Collecting Tendu leaves, and some piyar (chiraungi) Labour work for forest dept; Dahiya work (dispersing cowduug in fields and prepare it for next crops), reparing homes. Collecting fuel wood for rainy season.
June	Collecting tendu leaves and piyar, pit digging for plantation (forest dept). Dahiya work (spreading cowdung in fields to prepare it for Kharif cops). repairing homes, collecting fuel woods for rumy rainy season,
July	Preparing and sowing kharif crops (paddy, maize, arhar, urd, jwar, bajra, til), reparing homes.
August	Trans planting paddy
September	Transplanting paddy, collecting broom materials from forest and making brooms for home consumption for the entire year. Hunting, watching crops
October	Inter cropping, locking after crops, cleaning and pargetting walls with mud (mudding), cutting of paddy or Kharif crops.
November	Cutting paddy crops, Dhan dauri, Dhan Kutai, collecting fuel woods.
December	Dhan Katai, Dauri, looking after crops, sowing rabi crops, Labour migra-tion.

Note: This annual work schedule is applicable in all the study villages except Musahar Tali, because other villages are compara tive ly better endowed with agricultural fields and hence agriculture work is an integral part of village life (Photo 7 and 8)

Photo 7

Women of Karmabandh village sowing potato in their fields.

Rearing of animals, including goats in an important source of income generation.

Women enagaged in agricultural work.

From the table above, it is evident that women in the area are preoccupied all the year round either with agricultural activities or household management, there by not getting enough spare time for leisure.

Table 8: Seasonal Wark Calender of whom of Musahar Toli

Month	*Work*
Jan.-Feb.	Making pattals
March-April	Making pattals
May-June	Plucking Harre
July-Aug.	Labour work, forest food collection
Sept.-Oct.	Honey Collection, labour
Nov.-Dec.	Making Pattals, labour migration for cutting paddy, plantation work of forest Department.

The main occupation in Musahar is honey collection and making pattals. They also do labour work in the fields of nearby villages since they do not have their own land for agriculture.

Table 9: Seasonal Wark Calender

Hindi Months	*English Months*	*Employment Area*	*Aprox. days of employment*
Chaitra	15 Mar-14	Apr. Agri and Outdoor activities	18-20 days
Baisakh	15 Apr.-14 May	Collection of Mahua	15-17 days
Jayeshtha	15 May-14 June	Collection of Piyar and Plucking of Tendu Patta	20-25 days
Asharh	15 June-14 July	Agri. work	27-28 days
Shravan	15 July-14 Aug.	Transplanting, manuring and fencing	27-28 days
Bhadrapad	15 Aug.- 14 Sep.	Intercultural practices	20-22 days
Ashwin	15 Sep.- 14 Oct.	Ploughing	7-8 days
Kartik	15 Oct.- 14 Nov.	Ploughing and seeds sowing of rabi crops	25-27 days
Margshirsh	15 Nov.- 14 Dec.	Harvesting of paddy	15-20 days
Paush	15 Dec.- 14 Jan.	Threshing of paddy and storage	10-15 days
Mazh	15 Jan.-14 Feb.	Collection of wild Ber, Makoya and outdoor activities	10-12 days
Falgun	15 Feb.-14 Mar.	Outdoor activities	30 days

According to the calender, the intensity of work is more in months of Asharh, (15th June - 14th July) followed by Kartik (15 Oct. - 14 Nov.) and Jayeshtha (15 May - 14 June). The month of Bhadrapad and Ashwin (15 Aug. - 14 Oct.) are critical months during which very few job opportunities are available in the villages as well as outside the village. During this period, people tend to do some agricultural activities which necessarily does not effect the production of crops. During Phalguna and Chaitra (15 Feb. - 14 April), no work opportunity is available at all in the locality. Therefore, migration to adjoining urban centres takes place.

Decision-making abilities

This variable determines the actual empowerment situation of women in the area. How much power she has been given to take the decisions regarding various socio-economic issues. Data were collected through scoring by various seeds. They showed their own opinions for the statements as depicted under Table 10.

Table 10

	Subjects	*Decisions made by**		
		W	*H*	*B*
1.	Agricultural work	10	10	10
2.	Buying household and agricultural equipments	10	15	5
3.	Selling of cows, land and agricultural equipments	5	15	10
4.	Education of children	5	15	10
5.	Marriage of children	5	15	10
6.	Family planning	5	20	5
7.	Taking loan from a lender	5	15	10
8.	Selecting gram pradhan/political leader for development	-	25	5

W=Wife

H = Husband

B = Both

* Scoring by seeds.

The Table 10 - "Decision making abilities" of women was developed through an open group discussion. Different fields and areas of discussion were put before them and they had to tell their own opinion.

Findings show that most of the decisions were taken by their husbands. The consent of women is also taken into account in most of the cases.

But an important fact which was directly observed by the researcher was that women did not accept that most decisions were taken by their husbands only due to male dominance. It is also true that a woman's consent was limited only to take decision in favour of her husband. Rarely in some cases, when she is totally disagreed to the decisions taken by their husband, they have to compromise with her.

Table 11: Attitude of women towards social issues

	Issues	***Per cent age of total sample respondent (Positive scores)***
*1.	Women as housewife is as important as husband.	75
*2.·	Given education, opportunities, skills and necessary training in rural occupation, rural women can raise the family level of living.	100
*3.	Rural development efforts should identify and include role of women.	100
*4.	Women should participate in decision-making at family and village level issues.	75
*5.	Women should be paid equally for equal work as of men.	95
**6.	The choice of number of children or to adopt family planning should rest with husband.	85
**7.	Women should restrict themselves to home and should not come out to participate in social organisation.	15
**8.	Political participation is meant only for men.	15
**9.	One should restrict their social interaction to their caste only.	5

* Indicates agreed statements (positive)

** Indicates disagreed statements (negative)

The table depicts the information regarding attitude of women towards social issues. It was developed through an open discussion for which positive and negative scores were formed before the discussion. It was pre-checked before the use for better result.

All of them (100 per cent) strongly agreed that if a women is given education, opportunities, skins and necessary training, she can transform the rural life. Also, Rural Development efforts should include the participation of women. These statements were followed by the statement that women should be paid equally for the work performed by them (95 per cent). However, they disagreed on restricting social interaction of oneself to their caste only.

Table 12: Women's attitude towards girl child and family planning.

	Statement	*Percentage of total Sample respondent (Positive scores)*
**1.	There should be atleast two sons in a family.	100
**2.	The family having few children is better than more children.	50
**3.	If a family is having less girl child, family will remain happy.	100
**4.	A girl should learn household work instead of getting more education.	100
**5.	Family Planning operation reduces the body stamina.	100
**6.	A women should get operated instead of men for family planning.	100

** Indicates agreed statements.

Discussion about the family planning

To know about the opinion of women regarding family planning, an open discussion was held with the group of women. Previously selected statements were prepared to express their feelings of agreement or disagreement about the same.

Statement No. 1

'There should be at least two children in a family'.

All of them agreed to this statement replying in an old saying that "एक आंख को आंख नही कहायल जाला"

Statement No. 2

It is better to have more children than having few children in a family. Half of women (50 per cent) disagreed to this statement with a supporting statement that because our landholding is very small, it would be difficult to manage food and shelter to bigger family size. While 50 per cent of them were agreed to the statement by arguing that large family members share the work in the fields as well as can work outside to earn income, while small family will suffer from work load due to inadequate labour. According to them, small families with large land holdings are more sufferer than the family having more members with small land holding. बड़ी खेत हो के क्या होई जब करही वाला कोई नही बा

Statement No. 3

If a family is having less girl child, family will remain happy.

This was a positive statement and there was 100 per cent agreement to it with the following comments on dowry problem of the society. At the same time, they all agreed to taking dowry in their son's marriage.

It may be observed here that dowry has become a prevalent practice in such a remote and tribal area. Demand for dowry depends upon the land-holdings of the father. Dowry items include cash money, bicycle, watch, radio, silver chain etc. Decision of father in fixing the marriage of both boys and girls is mainly taken into account with a positive consent of the mother.

It was also observed that girl child is considered as a burden of the family and due to this reason, early marriages are prevalent in the area. They argued that a family having only male children definitely have a better socio-economic condition.

Statement No. 4

A girl should learn household work rather than get more education

This statement was also agreed (100 per cent) by all the women participating in the discussion.

They argue that a girl is a 'paraya dhan' and she should only get the primary education, so that she could read the letters only.

Statement No. 5

Family planning operation reduces the body stamina

All of them were having the mis-conception about the operation.

They all stated that operation reduces the body strength.

Statement No. 6

Women should get operated instead of men for family planning

Once again the prevailing gender discrimination clearly came to the forefront as they all agreed to this statement.

They argued that since operation reduces the strength of body, men should not get operated. They have to do hard work. Women still do not recognise that they are doing more labour intensive work in comparison to their male counterparts.

From the entire discussion, it can be generally concluded that the concept of gender discrimination is prevailing in the society of the study area and this is primarily because of lack of knowledge and exposure of women to the ground realities and facts.

OBJECTIVE - THREE

Health, Hygiene and Sanitation Condition of Women

To know about the health, hygiene and sanitation condition of women, Health P.R.A. was conducted in the area. Health P.R.A. is an application of the methodology of P.R.A. to learn from women about issues related to health. Following features were generated through health:

P.R.A.

* Crops grown in the area.
* Food product available from the forest.
* Foods taken daily; in festivals or on special occasions.
* Diets of pregnant and lactating mothers.
* Food security in critical periods.
* Immunisation and feeding practices among children.
* Faulty cooking methods.
* Drinking water facilities.
* Frequency of illness.
* Facilities/Methods of treatment of various illness.
* Local treatment and indegeneous medicines available; and
* Hygiene and sanitation condition.

Crops grown in the area

Two major activities in the study area are agriculture and gathering forest produce. Farming activity is generally done on subsistence basis.

The main crops of the area are paddy, wheat, gram, lentil, maize, sorghum, till, urd, moong, jowar, bajra, sugarcane and kerai. Paddy is the staple diet in the area and hence it is grown on a substantial basis, whereas other crops mentioned above are grown in smaller quantity.

Their daily diet consist of an average three meals a day which reduces in critical periods (Aug. - Sept.) to one or two meals a day. Only in rainy season, they get some vegetables. Their daily diet shows nutritional deficiency in protein and vitamin rich food. Sometimes, people hunt wild animals from forest for food. In rainy season, they get plenty of fishes.

Table 13: Various Crops grown and months.

A schematic representation of the various crops grown in the area during various months of the year is being depicted as following:

Crop/vegetables Rice, Wheat, Pulses, Potato, Fish, Forest animals

Months

Chait

Baishakh

Jyeshth

Aasadh

Savan

Bhadon

Kwar

Kartik

Agahan

Poush

Magh

Phalgun

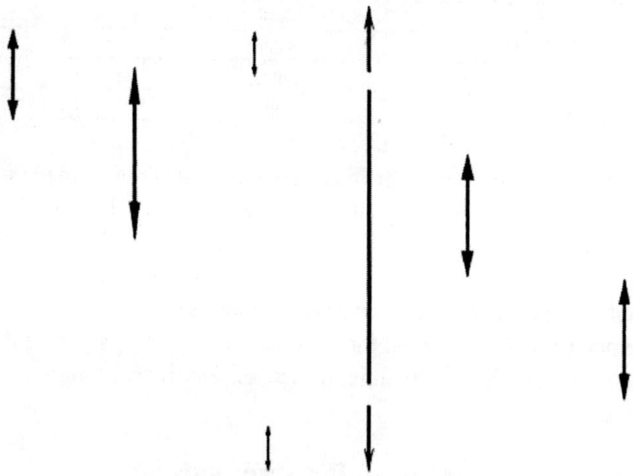

Vegetables are grown for domestic use only.

* when available.

Average yield per hectare is described as under. Crops are grown for the subsistence use only. If surplus are produced, sold when they need some cash money or bartered with other food items.

Table 14: Major crops and their average yields

Crops		*Yield (Qtl./hect)*
Major Crops		
1.	Paddy	12-14
2.	Wheat	10-12
3.	Maize	6-7
4.	Barley	10-12

(*Contd...*)

Pulse crops		
1.	Urd	2-3
2.	Gram	2-3
3.	Pea	3-4
4.	Lentil	2-3
Others		
1.	Jowar	2-3
2.	Bajra	2-3
3.	Kodo	2-3
4.	Sawan	1-2
5.	Ragi	1-2

Women are dependent on forest for food, fodder, medicines and raw materials for producing small items like leaf plates, brooms, baskets, cords etc. for their own use or for selling it in the markets. Apart from their dependence on forest lands as gatherers of forest produce, the women are also employed by forest department and contractors to work as unskilled labourers. Women provide fuel wood for household energy by gathering it from forest. They spend considerable time in such activity by walking long distances to procure these items.

Critical dependency on forest for subsistence

Women in the area prepared mobility charts which shows their movement of distances around their villages, for gathering fuel wood, forest products, raw materials or for foods.

Seasonal chart, social map and various open ended group discussions revealed valuable informations regarding forest produce which are categorised under following subheads:-

(i) Wild edible products.

(ii) Plants used for fibres.

(iii) Plants used to extract oil.

(iv) House building materials.

(v) Plants used in cordage, baskets and broom making.

(vi) Fuel.

(vii) Products used for miscellaneous purposes.

Table 15: Wild edible products

1.	Kandmul	Khaniya, Gainthi, Suran, Kushbagda.
2.	Vegetables	Karaila, Kunduru, Kheksa, Pidar, Van Sem.
3.	Jarigali Sag Green Leafy Vegetables	Karemua, Chakwad, Barwat, Jhiru, HilhuL, Khurput, Girni, Chaulai, Pathari etc.
4.	Trees Leaves	Koilar, Bahuar, Karemua
5.	Fruits	Tend, Makoi, Mahua, Piyar, Dhera, Ber, Bel, Katjamun, Sagaun, Sriphal, Gudsikari, Karaunda, Anola, Amola, Imli, Sakhu, Amla, Gular, Pidar, Girra, Kaiya, Gopali, Karmhara, Gamhar, Harre, Bahera etc.
6.	Forest animals and	Samar, Lamha, Kotar (Cheruka) Suar, Hiran, Birds Bhedar, Titar, Mor, Haril, Kalwari, Ledar, Varimurga, Bagaidi, Tital, Lava, Dhanesh, Katmurgi, Ashkol, Mahuar, Dhawan, Penduk Jhanghir, Shahi, Bater etc.
7.	Fish	Sehu, Silver, Bangur, Tengra, Garai, Moy, Jhinga, Patina, Sauri, Batasi, Chelhawa, Dhanwa, Dhawai, Bhakur, Karauchi, Nayan, Darahi, Bata, Aduar, Nekata, Ban, Kajar, Belgagra, Suitee, Barauna, Kusumha, Bulbula.
8.	Lasa of trees	Karmhara, Mango, Neem, Salai, Khair, Kharhar, Babul, Semar, Sakhu, Jigna*, Piyar

* Jigna is a kind of creeper which climbs on big trees. Villagers use. it to quench their thirst.

1.	Plants used for Fibre	Murra, Kathsahul, Katmahul, Mahulain, Beno, Karmhara, Kutchail, Palash, Chinanur. These fibres are Used for making ropes and fishing nets etc.
2.	Plants used to Extract oil	Koinadori, Keoniti, Neem, Sakhu, Rendi, Pili Sarason, Parvati, Karmhara, Mahua.
3.	House building Materials	Kadamba, Shisham, Dhaura, Siddha, Khaira, Sakhu, Kikar, Koira, Asna, Gurchi, Kumbi, Kadamb.
4.	Broom and Basket Making materials	Kus, Bagai, Jhoor, Lakkhu, Khajuri, Dhera, Bajrahi, Meur, Bans, Banvar.
5.	Fuel Plants*	Asidh, Bajrahi, Kharhar, Mamari, Katai

* Some times, they also cut shisham and sakhu for fuel consumption.

These people keep their houses warm and light with the plants mentioned above. The fuel collected from forest heats their cooking pot, lights the home, warm them during winter and saves them from attack of wild animals during night.

6. Plants used in medicine

Species	*Medicinal use*
Chirchiri	Jaundice and antidote to snake bite
Israul	Snake bite and fever
Salai	Stomach disorder
Karona	Fever
Silwaria	Dysentry, Dirrhoea
Biskanara	Relieving pain
Tend	Dysentry, Diarrhoea
Karihari	Rheumatism and Gout.
Padharis	Stomach pain
Kapuri	Cooling, Gonorrhoea and Other veneral diseases
Jartod	High fever
Patharchatti	Gonorrhoea
Karmhara	Blood Dysentry
Surpokha	Fever and snake antidote

Note:- Indigenous and traditional medicines which are obtained from forest herbs are described under the heading 'traditional medicinal practice'.

Besides all these plants, they collect honey, lac, wax, gum, resin etc. from forest area and definitely, these are critical input for their livelihood.

Table 16: Availability of Forest products throughout the year (month-wise)

	Minor forest Products	*Months*
1.	Mahua	Feb, March - April
2.	Piyar	Last April - Ist week of May
3.	Tendu leaves	1st week May - late June
4.	Harre	July-Sept, Feb -May
5.	Bahera	Feb. - April, July - Sept.
6.	Amla	April - May
7.	Kheksa	July - Sept.
8.	Kareli	Aug. - Sept.
9.	Kundrun	July - Sept.
10.	Gainthi	July - Jan.
11.	Khaniya	July - Jan.

(*Contd...*)

12.	Kusum	April - June
13.	Sakhu	April- May
14.	Bel	April - June
Fruits		
1.	Ber	Dec. - Feb
2.	Makoy	Dec. - Feb.
3.	Karonda	July - Sept.
4.	Imli	April - June
5.	Pidar	Aug. - Sept.
6.	Jamun	June - July
7.	Pipal	May - June
8.	Karmhara	May - June

Villagers living in the area depend on forest and tree products not only for foods, but also for other products. A detailed description of such dependency is being discussed below :-

1. Use of Forest for Food

A large number of forest products especially fruits, vegetables, different types of roots, wild animals and birds were reported to be used by local community for food purposes. Some forest foods are regular items in their diet, while others are used seasonally. At times, when the agricultural season keeps them very busy in fields, local people depend intensively on forest products. Certain forest products are exploited when extra cash is required and some at times of food shortages or crises.

(a) Root Products

Khania and Gainthi are the most important food products'obtained from the forest. These are the wild variety of yams available all year around and is used more intensively during the period of food shortage. Collecting these root products is the responsibility of women who travel long distances ranging from 8-10 Km. in forests for the same.

(b) Vegetables

Vegetables which are gathered from the forest include Karela, Kunduru, Kheksa, Pidar and Vansem.These are generally available during rainy season. Women said that they did not know how to preserve vegetables.

(c) Green leafy vegetables

Over nine varieties of green leafy vegetables are reported to be found in the forest. Out of these, Karemua, Chaulai, and chakwad sag are used intensively. Other green leafy vegetables are Barwat, Jhiru, Hilhul, Khurput, Girni and Pathari etc.

(d) Fruits

Over twenty five kinds of wild fruits were mentioned by women. Tendu, Mahua and Piyar were plentiful in the area and considered important both for consumption and as a source of extra income. Most of the popular fruits are listed in the Table 16 according to the season when they are available.

(e) Forest Animals and Birds

Wild animals like wild beer and wild pigs are considered a nuisance in the Naugarh area because they destroy their crops. This is due partly to the reserve forest area which is very close to their villages. However, wild animals like wild pigs, rabbits, samar, vanmurga; birds like Titar, Mar, Haril, Bater are mostly hunted by these villagers.

A list of animals and birds that are hunted for food can be seen in the Table 15. The use of wild animals for food is considered to be of great importance to the community as there are very few domesticated animals, which can be used for the same purpose. Animals which are domesticated include bulls, cows, buffaloes, goats, pigs, sheep and dogs. Continuous shooting and hunting of wild animal birds has tremendously reduced their number and availability.

(f) Gums and Resin

Gums of trees like Mango, Neem, Karmhara, Babul and Sakhu etc. are used by these villagers either for medicinal or for eating purposes.

(2) House Building Materials

Forests and trees make available logs of wood, bamboos, grass, fibres etc. required for constructing their huts and shelter. They do not recognise the value of scarce and highly demanded trees like shisham and sakhu but inspite of that, they use it for constructing their houses or even for fuel purposes. Plants used for cordage are Murra, Karsahul, Kathmaul, Mahulin, Beno, Karmhara, Kuchail and roots of palash.

(3) Fuel Wood and Fodder

The villagers of Naugarh block are dependent on forest trees for their fuel wood requirements. They collect it on a daily basis, while for rainy season-they collect it before mansoon sets in and store it for the purpose of fuel wood.

(4) Broom and Basket making materials

A number of plants are reported to be used for making brooms and baskets. In the month of Sept. - Oct., almost all the women of every household were seen making the brooms in large quantities. They prepare it for the whole year for household use only.

Traditional Medicine Practices

In Naugarh, the use of indigenous treatment and medicines is decreasing day by day. The information was obtained from various resource persons like aged women and the experts in tribal medicines, i.e. the 'Baiga' and individuals who had knowledge of plants having medicinal value and other economic uses. The data obtained from different localities/ villages were compared. People replied in an open ended discussi?~ that in the past, almost all kinds of diseases were cured by the indegneous medicines but today, it has reduced to three per cent only. In Aurawantand village, one man was found to practice in traditional medicines. On asking him about the range of illness/diseases which he was able to cure, he said that he had medicines for almost all kinds of illness and spoke about different kinds of mcdicines which he knew and which he uscd successfully. Further, he replied sarcastically that nowadays, villagers do believe on allopathic treatment which is being practised by 'Jholachap' doctors in Naugarh market. He listed some of the illnesses and the related medication he often recommended. Some of them are mentioned below.

Table 17: Medicinal plants and traditional medicinal practice with locally available plants and herbs:

1. पाताल कोहड़ा को पीसकर चीनी के साथ मिलाकर खाने से दाद ठीक हो जाता है।
2. पत्थरचट्टी (संजीवनी बूटी) आधा लीटर पानी में चूर कर (सुखाकर) चीनी में मिलाकर पीने से दाद ठीक होता है।
3. मुजुनी (जड़ी) 10 ग्राम पीस कर 10 ग्राम अजवाइन में मिलाकर 100 ग्राम तेल में सुखा लेते हैं। सर्दी–गर्मी में फायदा करता है।
4. सिहोर का पत्ता आंख में रोहुआ रोग ठीक करता है।
5. कहट की हड्डी छेद करके कमर में पहनने से बवासीर ठीक होता है।
6. ऊँट की हड्डी उभरते फोड़ा में पीसकर लगाने से ठीक होता है।
7. कछुआ की हड्डी जलाकर कपूर और तीसी के तले में फेंट कर लगाने से चर्म रोग ठीक होता है।
8. सलई का लासा पेट दर्द, उल्टी दस्त और ठण्ड लगने पर फायदा करता है।
9. कर्गहरा का लासा पेचिश में फायदा करता है। गाय के दही में शाम को भिगोया गया लासा फेंट कर सुबह पिलाते है।

10. बिसकनरा (जड़ी) को बीच से काटकर तेल डालकर तवे पर गर्म करके सेंकने से चोट ठीक होती है।
11. फनिहर सांप के तेल से धूप में मालिश करने से गठिया रोग ठीक होता है।
12. भालू का तेल गठिया रोग में काम करता है।
13. शेर का लिंग मीठे पान के साथ खिलाने से नामर्दी ठीक होती है।
14. मेंऊड़, आम की छाल, चीचीड़, मछुआ की छाल और पीला आकाश लता को 10 लीटर पानी में चूर कर (सुखाकर) पीलिया रोगी को स्नान कराया जाता है।
15. राम बांस गर्म करके गार करके सरसों के तेल में बराबर–बराबर मात्रा में मिलाकर दर्द में मालिश करने से फायदा होता है।
16. भटकइया की जड़, गरूच बौर, पीपल मुलेठी, काली मिर्च आदि पानी में चूरा कर आधी मात्रा हो जाने पर पानी को प्रसूति औरत को पिलाया जाता है।
17. फंकी पेट के लिए फायदा करती है इसको हर्रे? बहेरा, आंवला, सनाय, अजवाइन, काली मिर्च, जीरा, सोंठ, नमक को पीसकर बनाया जाता है।
18. शिलाजीत को पानी में घोल बनाकर पीने से खून साफ रहता है और स्वास्थ्य ठीक रहता है। (शिलाजीत का लासा चना भर मात्रा)।
19. सेहूण का पत्ता आग में हल्का भून कर एक चम्मच में गारके उसमें तड़का देकर सर्दी, जुखाम, निमोनिया में पिलाया जाता है।
20. गोह (जानवर) का तेल निमोनिया में मालिश किया जाता है और तीन बूंद पिलाया जाता है।
21. सीहोर का पत्ता पीसकर बुखार मे पिलाया जाता है।
22. करौंदा की जड़ ढ़ाई गण्डा मरीच (काली मिर्च) में पीसकर कपड़े में छानकर मियादी बुखार में काम करता है।
23. कुटज की छाल पीसकर 50 ग्राम कपड़े में छानकर मलेरिया में पिलाया जाता है।
24. अर्जुन की छाल ब्लडप्रेशर बढ़ने पर पिलाई जाता है।
25. हाथ का चमड़ा छोड़ने पर आठिल का डंडा लगाया जाता है।
26. महुआ का दूध रूई में करके दांत के मसूड़े में कीड़ी हो या दर्द हो तो उस जगह पर लगाया जाता है। महुआ का दातुन किया जाता है।
27. तेन्दू के पेड़ का खोराठी लेकर जहां भी कटा हो उसमें भर दे और उस जगह पर पानी पड़ना नहीं चाहिए घाव ठीक हो जाता है।
28. मलद्वार में कीड़े पड़े हो तो कुकरौधा का पत्ता मसलकर उसका पानी लगाया जाता है।
29. गुणमार की पत्ती जिसको सुगर हुआ हो उसे पिलाई जाती है।

Table 18: **Seasonal food calendar**

Months/items	*Rice*	*Wheat*	*Potato*	*Pulses*	*Onion*	*Vegetables*	*Fruits*	*Food from Other Season*	*Wild edible Foods*
Other Season Foods									
Chaitra (March-April)	6	-	4	2	2	Pumpkin	Guava	Fish	Mahua Piyar
Baishakh	5	8	3	1	1	Gourd	-	Fish	Tamarind
(April-May)									
Jyestha (May-June)	4	7	4	2	1				
Asharh (June-July)	3	5	3	2	1		Jamun	Fish	
Sravan (July-Aug.)	3	3	2	2	1	Beans		Fish	Pidar
Bhadrapad (Aug.-Sept.)	2	2	1	1	1		Papaya		Gainthi
Ashwin (Sept.-Oct)	1	2	1	1	-	Chichinda (Local name)		Fish	Khania
Kartik (Oct.-Nov.)	1	1	4	3	-	Potato			
Margshirsh (Nov.-Dec.)	8	1	2	1	-	Bitter gourd			
Poush (Dec.-Jan.)	10	-	2	2	1	Brinzal	Banana		Ber
Magh (Jan.-Feb.)	9	-	8	3	1	Pumpkin, brinjal, Tomato Ridge gourd			
Falgun (Feb-March)	8	-	8	4	1	Pumpkin, Brinjal, Tomato Ridge gourd			

Table 19: Preference Ranking of Foods Items

Food Items	*January*	*February*	*March*	*April*	*May*	*June*	*July*	*August*	*Sept.*	*October*	*November*	*December*	*Overall*
													Rating
Rice	xxxxx*	xxxx	xxxxx	xxxxx	xxxx	xxxx	xxxx	xxx	xxx	xx	xxxx	xxxx	1
Wheat	xx	x	x	xxx	xxxx	xxxx	xxxx	xx	xx	xx	x	x	2
Pulses	x	xx	xx	xx	xx	-	-	-	-	-	x	X	
Potato	xx	x	xx	xx	xx	xx	xx	x	-	-	x	xx	3
Green leafy Vegetables	-	-	-	-	-	xxx	xx	xx	-	-	-		
Onion	xx	xx	xx	xx	x	x	xx	x	-	-	x	x	
Milk	-	-	-	-	-	-	-	-	x	xx	x	x	
Oil	-	-	xx	xx	-	-	-	-	-		x	x	
Fruits** (Forest)	-	-	-	-	x	x	x	x	xx	-	-	-	
Meat** (Forest)	x	x	x	-	-	-	-	-	x	x	x	-	

* X shows number alloted by the women

** When available.

Dietary Practices

The morning diet is started with the stale food (the day old leftover food) as breakfast. Only two meals per day is the usual intake. But in critical months, it reduces to once in a day. The Ashwin month is critical for them because they hardly get enough to satisfy their hunger through -the staple foods. Sometimes, there is complete starvation for 2-3 days. During this period, they survive on 'gainthi', 'khaniya', 'mahua', some forest fruits etc. Women and children are the worst sufferers in the family. Usually women take their food at last, men are preferred to take the food first. This sequential pattern of eating, makes the woman most poorly fed member of the family.

It was an amazing fact that women of the study area also consume intoxicants of varied nature, which are being mentioned according to their relative intake in the following table.

Table 20

Intoxicants	*Male per cent*	*Female per cent*
Wine*	100	60
Ganja	60	-
Bidi	60	10
Surti	98	12
Tobaco	12	8
Beetle leaves	70	4
Gutka	100	2

* Wine is prepared from mahua, which is a major cash forest produce of the area. If it is not used for indigenous liquor preparation, but rather sold as a cash product, then it may fetch sizeable income to the community.

Dietary Practice of Pregnant and Lactating Mothers

As discussed earlier, both from observation and group discussion, it was found that the inhabitants of Naugarh block prefer to eat rice, chapati and pulses. It was also found that due to less availability of vegetables, green leafy vegetables, fruits and milk, their diets lack vitamins and minerals. Majority of the women were consuming less calories than what was required daily. Except cereals other food group was less than Recommended Daily Allowance. It may be revealed from the table which was scored by women themselves. Probing about the dietary practice in special groups like pregnant and lactating mothers, majority women replied that they did not take any special food in their diet during pregnancy, rather they decrease the amount of food during the same period. The women of the area were having the misconception that during pregnancy less amount of food should be taken. Besides these, they did not know about the importance of colostrum and fed (breast) their child three days after the delivery. No special weaning food was given to the children from the age of months to 18 months. They were given the same food which the adult people were eating. A gender discrimination was observed between a girl child and a boy child as a women and a girl child were consuming less quantity and a poor quality of food in their diet. This is due to the fact that men are considered superior than women in the area. Another example of gender discrimination was observed when men folk go to the forest and hunt the forest animals and consume them after cooking it in the forest itself.

Maternal and Child Care

It was found that women in the area have poor health and nutrition condition than men. The social customs and attitudes towards women adversely affects their nutritional and health status and access to health education. There was substantial maternal mortality and problem of anaemia among pregnant and lactating mothers due to poor nutrition. There was also a tendency not to report their own ailments or seek medical advice. Child bearing at the early age poses additional health problems for women.

It was found that children upto age of one year were forcibly made to lie on their stomach so that they are unable to move long distances, thereby giving there mothers ample time to do other household work.

But it was also found that this practice often leads to development of stomach ailments and vomiting tendency among children.

Method of Cooking

In participant observation, their faulty cooking practices was noticed. Faulty cooking methods are responsible for nutrient loss and thus for their poor health condition. Several faulty methods of cooking observed during study were as follows:

1. Vegetables are cut into smaller pieces, washed after cutting and cut much before cooking it.
2. Vegetables are cooked in open containers till its entire water gets evaporated. Over cooking of vegetables with more than the required amount of water is main cause of loss of vitamins and minerals.
3. Washing of rice and pulses 3-4 times before cooking with excess of water in an open container was also main cause of loss of water soluble vitamins.
4. Wheat flour was sieved before making chapaties.

The faulty methods of cooking destroys the micronutrients and some of the macro-nutrients of foods. They have the kitchen equipments like 'Dhengchi' (Pan), 'Tava', 'Chimta', 'Palta', 'Thali', 'Katori' etc. The food is cooked on chulha and fuel wood is taken from forest. Drinking water and water for cooking purpose were brought from a distance either from well or from handpumps. Traditional cooking utensils, collecting water and fuel wood from forests and preparing food on chulha takes more time and energy of women. Their eyes and lungs are also affected by smoke of chulha. These women feel that these problems are part of their life. Devices like pressure cooker, stove etc can reduce their burden but when asked about the same, they replied that 'yahan' to do joon lei roti ka jugad nahin ho pata, uske liye paisa kahan se ayega' (Here it is difficult to manage two times bread, how can we arrange other items).

Recipes prepared by them

Women prepare a limited variety of dishes in their diet. These were categorised under the following heads :

(1) Daily recipes.

(2) Festive recipes.

Daily recipes included the staple food materials which clearly indicates the lack of food items like fruits, vegetables and milk products.

During winter season, they consume rice, jowar, bajra etc. as staple food. Sometimes pulse is also available. Green leafy vegetables are available twicc or thrice a week while other vegetables like guard, pumpkin serve as supplement to their staple diet. During summer, wheat flour, barley flour etc. are staple food. Mahua, obtained from forest constitute a major part of their food requirement. During rainy seasons, green leafy vegetables are consumed which are obtained either from forests or are grown at their homes. Women generally cook the following recipes combinations (Table 21).

Table 21

1.	Sabji - Chawal	6.	Chawal - Namak (Salt)*
2.	Roti - Sabji	7.	Roti - Dal
3.	Dal- Chawal - Sabji	8.	Roti - Nonveg
4.	Dal- Chawal	9.	Roti - Namak
5.	Chawal - Dal - Sabji	10.	Roti - Pyaj (Onion) - Mirch etc.

* Namak is called as silchuran in local language and is prepared by mixing salt, garlic and chilli. It was found that they consume lots of chilli, salt and spices in their diet.

Festive Recipe

The dishes which are prepared occasionally in festivals, marriages etc are as follows:

Table 22

1.	Puri Sabji	6.	Pakodi
2.	Dal Puri	7.	Chura Dahi
3.	Chiraungi Roti	8.	Pua
4.	Khir	9.	Khichadi
5.	Nonveg	10.	Chura Dudh etc.

Table 23: Dishes prepared by Mahua

1.	Mahua + Tisi + Til (Dal)
2.	Mahua Roti
3.	Mahua Thenkua (Sweet Puri)
4.	Latta (Lapsi/Mixture of wheat flour + sugar + Mahua)
5.	Mahua + Chana + Sakhu seed (Roti)

From the various recipes mentioned under two broad categories, it can be well understood that the economic backwardness of the society is a major factor behind the malnutrition/under nourishment of the people, thereby giving rise a number of diseases/health problems.

Food Security in Critical Periods

There are number of edible products which are obtained from the forest, but mahua and piyar strongly support their subsistence as well as their economy. During critical periods of the year (Ashwin and Kartik), in most of the houses, only one meal during 24 hours is available and they depend entirely on forest. In such periods, Gainthi, and khaniya are major food items a fleshy tuber of a creeper found during and after rainy season. Gainthi is much bitter than bitter gourd, so it can not be consumed alone, therefore, it is mostly consumed with Mahua (roasted or boiled in water after peeling and slicing into small pieces and then put into flowing water for 12-18 hrs.) Khaniya which is found in scarcity is consumed directly after peeling. Besides these, some green leaves like mustard and pumpkin leaves also supplement their diets.

The villagers consume a variety of seasonal items (listed in Table18) of food gathered from different sources depending upon their availability from the market. It also depends on their purchasing power which is quite meagre. Since rice is the major ingredient of their foods, the unavailability of the same could not be compensated by other food items. The availability of rice starts declining during Chaitra and Baishakh resulting in sharp reduction in food intake during subsequent months.

In recent years, with environmental degradation, availability of wild food from forest shrank to a large extent and became negligible. Women who are the main gathered of food are forced to walk longer distances for the same. Hence, poor people in that area were either forced to reduce their consumption of wild food by going hungry or buying them from the market by generating additional income. However, livelihood opportunities have declined in recent years. It is fact of their life that mahua, tendu leaves and piyar (Chiraungi) contributes 50 per cent of their economy. But they face lots of problem regarding collection and sale of these minor forest products.

Collection of Mahua

Due to degradation* of Mahua trees there is continued scarcity of mahua flowers and fruits for both the community and wild animals like bear. Mahua is sold in market for ₹ 15-16 a Kg. in the season. They barter dry and wet mahua to get essential food commodities. In season, they exchange one Kg. rice for one Kg. of mahua. Mahua supports livelihood of local communities in three ways.

- For providing subtistence needs of food, wine and medicine.
- As a source of income.
- As saving to be encashed to meet contingencies.

As stated earlier, their economic condition is so poor that they cannot save mahua to sell it during the off season which might enable them to earn two times more money than during the season. However, some NGOs working in the area are thinking to establish Mahua and Chiraungi bank for their livelihood support.

Mahua is used in different forms and on different occasions as edible items:-

1. Mahua is used as a staple food. They consume its fruit after boiling it in water either as such or with rice and chapati.
2. Fruit's seed called as koina is also eaten by them.
3. Mahua is served as medicine for the treatment of different diseases.

---

* Although separate Mahua trees are allotted to every person by their own understanding but sometimes it became a matter of quarrel between them as a result it has also been seen that villagers go to forest in night to collect mahua. They light some fire to watch it clearly and sometimes accidentally forest catches fire and remained lit for 15-30 days continuously.

4. Oil of koina serves the purpose of cooking medium as well as massage of infants and children.
5.* They prepare a local liquor from the mahua.
6. It is a major source of income for them.
7. On special occasions like some festivals or marriages, the mahua is mixed with wheat flour and sugar and deep fried in mahua oil to prepare sweet puri.

It was found that liquor consumption had adversely affected the villagers' health. Although the health hazards of liquor consumption was known to villagers, yet its consumption continued unabated.

Collection of Tendu leaves

Tendu leaves collected from the forest, support their seasonal earnings which sustained them during rainy season.

One bunch or gaddi consisted of 60 tendu leaves. One person was able to pluck 200 such gaddis in one day and sold it ₹ 30 per 100 gaddis of Tendu leaves. During the season of Tendu leaves (May-June), each and every member of a family is engaged for leaf collection. Women described the scene in following manner.

Case Study regarding collection of Tendu Leaves - Table 24

तेन्दू पत्ता काफी सुबह ही तोड़ा जाता है। चूँकि हमारे पास घड़ी नही है, इसलिये कई बार हम लोग रात को ही जंगल निकल जाते है। अंधेरे में कई बार पहाड़ो पर चढ़ते समय गिर जाते है, लेकिन फिर उठकर चल देते है, खून बहता रहता है। इस समय हम लोगे को तेन्दू का एक–एक पत्ता में पैसा दिखाई देता है। हर आदमी सोचता रहता है। कि वह जितना मेहनत कर लेगा उसको उतना पैसा मिल सकता है। जिससे कुछ महिने तो अच्छा काम चल सकेगा। रात भर बैठकर पूरा परिवार या तो घर या जंगल में ही बैठकर गड्डी बनाते है। आग जलती रहती है। (जंगल से ही लकड़ी काटकर उसको उजाले के लिये जलाया जाता है। आंखे मूंदी जाती है। मगर हाथ चलते रहते है उस पर भी सरकार पूरा पैसा नही देती कभी कम रेट पर ही बेचना पड़ता है।

वे महिलायें जिनके छोटे बच्चो है और भी मुश्किल का सामना करती है। तब बच्चे को या तो सास या अन्य छोटे बच्चो के सहारे छोड़ जाती है जिससे उनके बच्चों के रख रखाव ओर खान–पान पर बुरा असर पड़ता है। ऐसी हालत में उनकी धारणा यह बन जाती है कि परिवार में अधिक सदस्य होने पर आददनी बढ़ सकती है।

* Mahua liquor is commonly consumed both by men and women in large quantity. More than 50 per cent of women were found to consume mahua liquor.

Collection of piyar (Chiraungi)

Chiraungi is also a valuable product of Naugarh forest, which supports their livelihood to some extent. They collect the whole seed from the forest in the season of April-May. Whole seed is sold at the rate of ₹ 60 a Kg. or they barter it one Kg of piyar to 7 Kg of rice.

The local mahajans purchase chiraungi in its crude form (i.e. the entire seed). They then process it and sell the final product in the market at a price which is generally 3-4 times the cost price. There is lack of storage facility for the product in the block, as a result it can not be retained to be sold during off season when it can fetch higher prices. Also, the collector (especially women) can fetch a better price if they sell the product after grinding.

Due to degradation of forest, the production of piyar is decreasing day by day. Still they do not have any concept of planting new saplings or saving trees.

Some nutritions and delicious preparations of Chiraungi seeds are consumed by them as a special recipes like Chiraungi roti, Chiraungi puri, and Chiraungi lapsi.

Collection of Dhak leaves for pattal making: Case of Musahar

Musahar have very little or no land they have the most pitiable condition in the area. They do labour work, collect honey, tendu leaves, mahua, piyar and making pattals for their livelihood. Sometimes they have to migrate outside for labour work.

Pattal making is the main occupation of the people of Musahar, but are facing lots of problem for the same. Pattal is sold at the rate of ₹ 8 for 100 pattal. Approximately, they make 500-600 pattal in a day. Ohak' leaves are used to make the pattals which are plucked from the forest in the months of Ashwin to Phalgun. It's very tedious job and earning from the same is not sufficient to meet their daily requirements. They feel great difficulty in selling it in market because the demand for leaves plates is low due to the introduction of plastic plates. They get low price for the immensely hard work.

The women in the area demanded for press machine to make pattal dona. The machine can reduce the hard labour work and they will get fair price of dona pattal. They can make as many as one thousand pattal in an hour through the machine for which they are spending at least one and a half day. They also demanded for proper 'theka' and market to sell their honey products. They have to sell it at the price of ₹ 20-25 per Kg. However, it can fetch as high as ₹ 80-100 a Kg. if they have their own 'contract'.

Collection of Ber and Amla

Ber and Amla are collected in the season by these villagers and is sold either in dried or fresh form.

In the season, a family consisting of 4-5 members can collect 30-40 Kg fresh ber. After drying it (called khatai in local dialect), it is exchanged with equal amount of pulses of either lentil, pea or gram. From one kg. of fresh ber 300-350 gms. of dried product is obtained. Likewise, amla is collected in season and sold at rate of ₹ 4-5 per kg. A family can collect 150-200 kg. fresh Amla in a season.

Drinking Water Facilities in the area

It was observed that relatively small quantity of water was available in the area in limited sources. Major source of drinking water was handpumps, which were installed by the government in the area. Other sources are pond, wells and chuwan.

Hand Pump

A limited number of handpumps were found in the study villages. As shown in social and resource map, one or two handpumps have been digged up for the entire population of village. Some handpumps were not functioning due to lack of proper site selection, planning, poor handling and care.

Ponds

Ponds were found as natural water source in these villages. These are storage of rain water and ground water and are situated near the hills. It's water does not serve the drinking purpose but is used for washing clothes and taking bath. In summer, it's water irrigate the fields through it's high flow.

Wells

One or two wells have been digged in each village, but it is never used for drinking purpose due to its muddy water.

Chuwan

It is the important source of water for villagers in almost all seasons. It is like a pit where seepage water gets collected. This water is used for washing clothes or taking bath and for drinking of livestock. Villagers sometimes also use this water for drinking, but this is very much hazardous for their health.

Hygiene Practices

Hygiene deals with both the healthy individual as well as healthy community. Prevalence of malnutrition among people is not only due to dietary insufficiency but certain other factors are also responsible for the same. Poor hygiene and sanitation is one of them. For proper health and protection against infectious diseases, maintenance of good personal hygiene and environmental sanitation is very necessary. The various factors responsible for proper sanitation and hygiene are as follows:

1. Personal

It was observed that men, women and children do not take bath daily. They do not wash their hands with water before preparing, serving or eating food. For prevention against contagious diseases, frequent washing of hands is essential. The nails of women and children were found to be neither cut properly nor clean. The hair of children remain dirty. In some children, flag sign of hair was also observed. Children were not cleaning their teeth and tongue daily. Among majority of women, headache and eye problem (redness and pain) was prevalent. It was not only due to dietary insufficiency, but poor hygiene practices were also responsible to enhance their severity. Even after sneezing, they do not wash their hand. Mothers never bother to wash or launder clothes even after they are wet by children's urine and vomit. No proper place was fixed for urination and defecation of children. Therefore, poor sanitation has become part of their life.

2. Environmental

People use to wash clothes collectively. Generally, the housewives do not have any separate management for food and clothing of diseased person. There was no proper management for the drainage of waste water which leads to breeding of mosquitos and flies. These pests carry and spread pathogens in nearby locality and thus serve as a contributing factor for creating health problems like malaria, viral infections etc. Besides, ventilation arrangement was not proper leading to insufficient light and sunshine, causing damp and dark condition in rooms. Household wastes were not disposed properly and generally thrown in the backcourt of the house causing unpleasant odours and growth of pathogens.

The practice of keeping livestock inside house causes transmission of diseases through flies (which are produced and increased in their number due to livestock excreta sitting on food materials and through walking barefoot).

Hazards of Water Pollution

Water was found to be polluted with dissolved and in dissolved impurities like minerals and suspended particles like sand, mud, rotten leaves and microscopic plants and animals. Another cause of water pollution was human activities like washing of face, hand, feet and washing themselves after defecation. Animals and livestock are found to serve as an important agent of water pollution. In addition, detergents, soap, dirt, dust, dyes and pigments from clothing also contaminate water. Use of this water either for drinking purpose or consuming throughfood was found to play a major role in prevalence of health hazards.

Skin diseases were also found to be prevalent which may be due to polluted water and other deficiency. Among respiratory diseases, majority of people were found to be suffering from whooping cough. The incidence was highest among infants, pre-schoolers and old aged people. The main causative factor was lack of immunisation. It was more pronounced in winter season due to their unhygienic life pattern, poor sanitation and low socio-economic status. The bacilli causing whooping cough spreads quickly to others.

Sanitation Facilities

Sanitation involves proper disposal of waste and other refuse from house, disposal of body waste, control of household pests like mosquitoes, flies, rats and cockroaches etc. In the surveyed area, normally the disposal of waste water and refuse is not proper. Only one sewer was generally made in one corner of the courtyard with an outer opening into a small space.Thus, sewage water gets accumulated outside which catalyses the breeding of mosquito and flies.

Disposal of Body Waste

For disposal of body waste, no arrangement was observed inside house. Elder members of family generally go to forest or farms, far from their houses for disposal of body waste while for toddlers, any place of house (even kitchen) can be used for execution of faeces or urine. The distance covered to dispose off body waste varies from season to season. In rainy season, people used to go in nearer plots around the village while in summer and winter they walk about 100-150 meters away from village.

Arrangement of Clean Air

As it is observed that the inhabitants of this area are not aware of importance of clean air so they do not make any special provision for air ventilation in their rooms. It may be due to the reason that most of their time is spent outside their house. Even then a small opening of about one square feet is provisioned in upper side of the central wall. Normally the height of door was about 5 feet which neither give comfort nor proper air and lighting.

Generally, the walls of their houses get cracked. Attack of termites were also observed on it. Livestock management inside the house was observed which is also responsible for reducing the provision of clean air.

Diseases and Ailments

Sickness, ailments and diseases are part and parcel of life of a community. Health related intervention by its nature can exercise more spectacular and perhaps profound influence on this aspect of life of people. Therefore, it becomes necessary to make a factual survey of the situation as thoroughly as possible.

While probing about the health problems which these local women suffered from, they listed out the following:

1. Fever
2. Cold
3. Body-ache
4. Tuberculosis
5. Night Blindness
6. Malaria
7. Leprosy
8. Filaria
9. Red eyes (Cunjectivitis)
10. Ear Problem
11. Semua (white spots)
12. Measles on the face
13. Cancer
14. Dermatitis
15. Diarrhoea
16. Cholera
17. Tumour
18. Anaemia
19. Leg Trembling
20. Leg swelling
21. Whooping Cough
22. Pneumonia
23. Venereal diseases
24. Hernia
25. Dysentry

Among these diseases, fever, malaria, diarrhoea, dysentry, headache and pneumonia are most common in the area and they sometimes lead to death also. In general both men and women do not think that there is any serious health problem. However, some women mentioned that they keep losing weight and suffering from severe headache, but do not know the reason behind it. Fever is a common problem of the area and takes longer time to get cured (sometimes for a month also) thereby leaving them extremely weak. Many children have eye infection and running nose. Diarrhoea is common during rainy season.

Time-line about incidents of death in the villages were also it collected.

Table 25: Deaths caused by major diseases during last five years

1. Village : Nunwat

Year	*Cause*	*Deaths*
1995	Cholera	3
1999	Delivery death	1
1999	Snake biting	1

at present (till July 2000) there is one case of cancer, three cases of T.B., one case of polio, three case of leprosy and two cases of Asthma.

2. Village: Aurawantand

Year	*Cause*	*Deaths*
1998	Tuberculosis	1
1998	Snake biting	1
1993	Unknown	1

at present (till July 2000) there is one case of mental disturbance and one case of polio.

3. Village : Semar

Year	*Cause*	*Deaths*
2000	Cancer	1
2000	Delivery Death	1

at present (till July 2000) there is one case of polio and one case of goitre.

4. Village: Musahar

Year	*Cause*	*Deaths*
1995	Asthma	1

at present there are two cases of T.B. Patient.

5. Village: Shahpur

Year	*Cause*	*Deaths*
1997	Cancer	1
1999	T.B.	1
2000	Delivery Death	1

at present there are four cases of leprosy.

Time-line as under Table 25 shows that during 'last five years (1995-2000), four women died during delivery. In case of delivery, they often call local daies who are neither expert to handle efficiently the complicated cases nor provided with sterilised and safe instruments.

Medical Facilities for treatment

As far as medical agencies available for treatment is concerned, there are four major agencies through which they seek medical treatment

1. Government agencies i.e. Govt. hospitals or P.H.C's
2. Private Practitioners.

3. Indigenous Practices.
4. Occult practitioners or local priests.

For each and every village, one community worker has been appointed by state govt., but they never visit these villages. Women replied in a question that they were never given iron and folic acid tablets. There is no facility for regular health checkup of a pregnant woman. Children were occasionally immunised on these health centres.

In case of serious problems, villagers approach to local priests but they make the case more complicated. In such situation, they go to private practitioners at Naugarh block or to Primary Health Centres. The private practitioners sit in the block, are not registered doctors and they exploit these villagers by charging higher prices and providing improper treatment. These villagers can never think of going to Varanasi or Robertsganj even in most severe cases due to their poor economic condition and poor transportation facilities. Women and children are the worst sufferer in the area. Women have to face dual problem in these situations as they tend to conceal their problems as long as possible on one hand, and on the other, express their inability to discuss their health problems in front of male doctors. Consequently, they are forced to live a miserable life with deteriorating health. Views of women regarding their preference of medical agencies for their treatment are summarised as under:

Table 26: Preference to medical agencies

	Agencies	*Preference**
1.	Government Agencies i.e. PH.C. or Govt. Hospitals	6
2.	Private Practitioners	8
3.	Indigenous Practices	2
4.	Local priests or Occult Practitioners	4

* Scoring was done on a scale of 10.

This table brings out an interesting fact that compared to such traditional agencies 'as occult practitioners and indigenous practitioners modern practitioners of medical treatment are preferred first. Villagers do have faith in local priests, but very often, these practices make the condition worse than before.

OBJECTIVE - FOUR

Identification of needs/problems and their classification in order of priority as suggested by participants

In various meetings and open discussion with male and female groups, villagers expressed their views about local problems. All contributions were accepted without criticism and listed on register or on large sheets of chart paper pasted on mud walls. Discussion with both men and women group helped in serving the dual purpose of cross-checking and testing the reliability and validity of data and also seeking gender perspective about the identified problems.

The researcher helped the villagers to generate the ideas; similar ones were grouped together, repetition eliminated and casual relationship between problem were discussed. Sometimes, researcher felt that people do not realise the problems and needs because they have not exprienced the possibility of its fulfilment. In such cases, closed non-participant observation helped the researcher to seek their needs and problems. Further date collected from them was shard back with them individually or collectively to minimise the bias and to collect truely representative data.

List of the problems can be broadly classified in to five major categories. Priority-wise, their classification are as following:-

I. Problem of food insecurity.

II. Economic problems.

III. Infrastructural problems.

IV. Social problems.

V. Miscellaneous problems.

Classification of Problems:

I. PROBLEM OF FOOD INSECURITY.

(A) Problems related to agriculture

1. Majority of the farmers suffer from shortage of farm land and small farm size due to which agricultural production is low.
2. Farming is dependent on rainfall and there is no other source of water in the study villages except Aurawantand. Irregular rainfall also cause less production.
3. Wild animals are a problem in the area. The crops and domestic animals are attacked and destroyed by these animals.
4. Low soil fertility.
5. Traditional crops with low returns.

6. The land these farmers have around their homes, is too small to plant trees for horticulture or seasonal vegetables. There are also problems of irrigation water and safety from domestic animals as they are not tied with ropes and they spoil the seedlings of these crops.
7. Most of them have a limited knowledge about modern agricultural practices. The crops are attacked by different pests and diseases. They also do not have inputs like improved seeds, fertilisers and modem farming implements.
8. There is no concept of cash cropping, mixed farming or horticultural activities.
9. The worst part of livelihood is from Ashwin to Kartik (Oct. to Nov.) months when there is no agricultural production. They have to depend upon the forest products for their survival.
10. Problem of water logging in Semar village.
11. Need of Diesel pumping sets in Aurawantand village.
12. They use chemical fertilisers in their fields. Since it needs to be supplemented with proper irrigation, the lack of the same is slowly degrading the soil and thereby adversely affecting productivity.
13. Small land holding size prevent farmers from going in for modern agricultural equipments. High cost of these equipments prevent the farmers to possess and use it.

(B) Problem of Food Scarcity

1. Food shortage in the month of Quar - Kartik.
2. Low production of milk fro:n animals inspire of large number of cows in the area.
3. Shortage of fodder for grazing animals.
4. Animals are not tied, so that they sometimes graze the crops of their owners and plants of kitchen garden.
5. No concept of Kitchen Garden due to
   - Unawareness
   - Traditional belief
   - No land near their homes.
   - Lack of protection of plants from grazing animals due to improper fenced yards.
   - Because some houses are built on the stones, they are unable to grow vegetable or fruit plants.

6. Due to degradation of forest, they have to move longer distances for collection of forest food items.
7. Due to scarce availability of food they suffer from many malnutritional diseases.

II. ECONOMIC PROBLEMS

1. Problem of indebtedness.
2. Problem of unemployment.
3. No concept of saving.
4. Problem of less wage earnings due to lack of proper market and dependence on middlemen.
5. Lack of adequate job opportunities and cottage industries for income generation.

III. INFRASTRUCTURAL PROBLEMS

1. Problem of education (especially for girls).
2. Lack of proper approachable roads to the village and within the village.
3. Absence of Primary Health Care Centres.
4. Problem of conveyance/Transportation.
5. Lack of market nearby their villages.
6. Problem of toilet. They use to go to forest or places away from their home. Women especially face this problem and the problem is more severe in the rainy season.
7. Lack of safe drinking water.
8. Due to poor economic condition, inhabitants of some villages are unable to possess the diesel pumping sets which are required for irrigation, essential for better crop production.
9. Non-availability of electricity in the area. Provision was made by the Govt. to supply electricity to the area. Electricity poles and cables were also supplied but since the power supply was not provided, the essential equipments mentioned above were also stolen by localities.
10. Non-availability of lady doctors in the villages.

IV. SOCIAL PROBLEMS

1. Dowry problem.
2. Educational problems, illiteracy of women.
3. Overburden of work of women folk.

4. Secondary status of women and less say in decision-making regarding major household issues.
5. Prevalance of casticism in the area.
6. Inefficiency or lack of interest of gram pradhan and block pramukh towards development work for their villages. They are overburdened by their political commitments rather than social commitments.
7. Problem of misuse of allocated funds by gram pradhans or block pramukh.

V. MISCELLANEOUS PROBLEMS

1. Problem of mosquitoes in rainy seasons.
2. Problem due to forest degradation.
   - Women have to cover long distances for fuel wood collection.
   - Increasing population and deforestation is catapulting the problem.
   - No concept of plantation of new saplings existing.
   - Due to unavailability of forest officials, deforestation is going on.
   - Forest animals intruding in their fields and damaging their crops.
3. Unawareness about developmental programmes about their own welfare.

Although a number of NGOs are functional in the area, and are said to be working in the field of imparting primary education, yet their contribution towards the overall development of the area remains to be seen. Very often, these NGOs tend to establish their supremacy over their counterparts and thereby grab more developmental funds from the donor agencies. Such NGOs also try to woo the localities by giving them financial allurement. However, this is not a generalised observation because it came to the notice of the researcher that a society being run by Christian missionaries has tried to provide financial assistance to the people to invest in their occupation for greater prosperity. The developmental programmes implemented by Govt. agencies have proved to be a non-starter. No special programme targeting women was successfully launched because of male functionaries in the monitoring and execution of such programmes. If such development programmes are monitored and executed by females, then its success will be far reaching.

Awareness among women is slowly developing, but what is more important is to bring together these women folks and try to create a conducive atmosphere where they can openly share their views and problems.

OBJECTIVE - 5

Participatory Intervention Programme

Participatory Intervention Programme takes place beyond initial education. It is a life long process of further enhancing human empowerment for achievement of better and higher quality of life. It was initiated in the three villages among the interested women groups, with the following objectives:

1. Imparting literacy skills to illiterates.
2. Organisation of women groups and creating a sense of dignity and confidence to tackle their problems with a sense of solidarity to work together.
3. To create an awareness regarding health, nutrition, hygiene and sanitation etc.
4. To help them to think systematically about their own needs and problems and plan their lives accordingly.
5. To sustain their interests throughout the study period and gather informations with all their participation.
6. To develop the leadership ability among them.

Plan of Programme:

1. Formation of women groups

Concept of formation of informal women groups was new to the area, as there were no such informal groups in existence. Groups were formed in three villages namely: (1) Nunwat, (2) Aurwantand and (3) Karmabandh

Initially, all women of these villages joined the group, but later on, some of them could not continue it due to several reasons like caste-wise stratification of the area, unwillingness of males and greater work force participation of women etc. However, 45 women willingly got associated with the group. Village-wise distribution of the women were as follows:

1.	Nunwat	-	12 Women
2.	Aurawantand	-	13 Women
3.	Karmabandh	-	20 Women
	Total	-	**45 Women**

2. Identification of needs and resources

As stated earlier, literacy programme was initiated on the extensive demand of women. Further, problems and needs were analysed in different P.R.A.

sessions. Recognising the felt need of these women, several awareness generation programmes were implemented like :-

Promoting them to increase the consumption of vegetables; Preservation of locally available forest fruits and vegetables; Introducing new recipes based on locally available food; and Awareness regarding hazards of poor hygiene and sanitation on their health.

Resource identification is essential to reach the goals of functional literacy programme. Resources to conduct the programmes were perceived by focus group discussion by the local women. It was categorised as inputs in hand and inputs required to be procured, which varied according to the programme and the topics. Resources needed are described as in the Table 26 :-

Table 27

Programmes	***Resources***	
	Available	***Required***
1. Literacy Programme	Place	Slate, pencil, chalk, books, Blackboard
2. Growing vegetables and fruits.	Land, organic fertiliser, sickle etc.	Seeds, charts
3. Preservation of local foods	Locally available tubers like Khania and Gainthi turmeric and Achar masala Chulha and Kitchen Equipments.	—
4. New Recipes		
a. Chura Matar	Chura (Parboiled rice) Pea, onion, oil, potato, salt, turmeric, chulha, kitchen equipment.	—
b. Mung chila	Mungdal, oil, salt, garlic, chulha, kitchen equipment.	—
c. Palak and methi roti and sag	Palak, methi, wheat flour, chulha, kitchen equipment.	—
5. Awareness regarding Hygiene and Sanitation	—	Charts, posters, focus group discussion, case studies

Participatory Implementation of the Programme

The programme was a flexible and participatory in nature, i.e. it could be subjected to change as and when the need arised. As the programme was developed by the participants, it gained their trust, confidence and commitment.

Participation of women in an intervention programme of literacy.

Participation of Women in an intervention Programme of literacy.

Photographs show tangible results of the seeds distributed and sown in their kitchen graden.

Photographs show tangible results of the seeds distributed and sown in their kitchen graden.

Literacy Programme

It comprised of the knowledge of primers, matras, word making and making simple sentences.

One alphabetic book named "Vikas Hindi Balpothi", one slate and pencils were distributed to each woman for the purpose.

The programme was implemented for six months. Date and time was decided by the women, which varied according to seasonal work load of the women. Sometimes, classes were taken in night also due to their busy day schedule (Photo 9, 10 and 11).

Results

1. Regarding knowledge of the primers (अ...ह) , 95 per cent women could read and write the primers. However, 20 per cent women (9) were difficulty to write ऋ, अं
2. Regarding word formation, the most difficult area of second primer 'a the usc of conjuct j cg. in words likc चर्चा, प्रधान 60 pcr ccnt of women were able to write and read simple words like माला, घर, नाली etc.
3. 10 per cent (4) of the women were found competent enough to make sentences and read and write it.

Awareness generation regarding higher intake of fruits and vegetables

It was observed that the diet of these people lack vegetables (specially green leafy vegetables). Ignorance regarding importance of vegetables and fruits and lower availability are the main reasons for less consumption of the same.

Importance of vegetables was discussed through on open group discussion. Women were convinced about the same. Some seasonal seeds of palak, methi, chaulai, papaya, beans, cucurbits were distributed to these women to try them out in the lands near to their houses (Photo 12 and 13 show the tangible results of the seeds distributed and sown in their Kitchen garden).

Results were found much encouraging, except in some cases. The women described the following problems they faced during cultivation:-

1. They do not have much land area near their houses.
2. Problem of irrigation was acute and they found it difficult to bring water from a distance.
3. As their fields were not properly fenced, domestic animals caused damage to their plantations.

4. Some houses were built in the rocky area, so their soil was not good for vegetables cultivation.

Both tangible and intangible results could be assessed from the above efforts. Green leafy vegetables like palak and methi, tomato, radish, turnip and papaya were successfully grown in the area which rose the self-confidence, satisfaction and enthusiasm among group women.

Programme of Cooking and Preservation

Researcher found some locally availables food materials which could be preservated in the form of pickle, badi etc. These villages produced large quantities of white pumpkin in the month of February, Amla in the month ofApril-May, Khaniya and Gainthi in month of July- Jan. These products were tried out to make badi, murabba and achar with the help of locally available preservatives like turmeric, salt, gram masala, sugar and vinegar.

These women are now recognising the importance of preservation of food items and programme was widely accepted and gained remarkable achievement. Women in the area later on ascribed their interest to make these products on large scale for marketing, with supply of raw material to them.

In the month of January, the researcher found the mass consumption of chura (parboiled rice) in the area. They took it in milk or curd. Demonstration of preparing chura matar was done which was greatly liked by these women. The women promised to prepare this new recipe on the occasion of Khichadi (Makar Sankranti).

Likewise, the seeds of Methi and palak which were distributed earlier, were ready in month of Feb. The roti and sag of these green vegetables and recipes like mung chila and mug gughari were demonstrated to them. As these were never prepared before, it proved a great acceptance (Photo - 14).

Awareness generation regarding hazards of poor hygiene and sanitation condition.

In different participatory sessions it was observed that the inhabitants of the area lack knowledge regarding the importance of personal and environmental cleanliness. In different meetings, group discussion were held, telling them about sanitation, hygiene, benefits of ventilated houses, clean water, personal cleanliness and use of trench latrines. They were also told about the health problems caused by consuming stale foods.

It was found that the message was clearly understood by them and they are trying to change their habits towards a more hygienic and healthy life.

Women of Nunwat Village preparing 'mung chila' and 'mung gughari' in an intervention programme of cooking (Photo No.14)

Strength, Weakness, Opportunities and Limitations of the intervention programmes (SWOL Analysis)

SWOL analysis provides a framework which allows for group analysis of issues i.e. interventional programmes. Four categories (Strength, weakness, opportunities and limitations) in the framework were used to examine, define, discuss and record the issues.

Purpose of the tool was to provide a framework of a given programme, encourage input from them and to gather qualitative information.

Purpose of the tool was described to women; description of categories like strength, weakness, opportunities and limitations were explained to them and they were told to express their own views.

Strength

1. The programme was according to the needs of women in the area.
2. It was run in the leisure time period of women.
3. Frequent visit to the research area, created a sense of belongingness and faith among local women.
4. Due to the distribution of slate, pencil and book, they could practice to write primers at their home also.
5. Local women themselves decided the place of learning in each village, where they could learn without any hesitation and interference of men and children.
6. Beside the literacy programme, some other awareness generation programmes held their interests throughout the period.
7. Almost all age group of women showed their interest to become literate and became the group member which created a learning atmosphere in the villages.
8. Local language was used to teach them which developed a better rapport among them.
9. Sometimes, local song session was also held to generate their interests.
10. Dropout school girls were also allowed to attend the group activities.

Weaknesses

1. Due to heavy work load, sometimes women could not spare much time which caused irregularity in the programme.
2. Due to severe casticism, programme had to be implemented in two separate tolas in one village itself which consumed more time and energy for the same purpose.

3. Heavy work-load during day time and non-availability of light at night hindered them to practice at their own home.
4. Male members sometimes used to make fun of them.
5. Researcher was not able to stay in the village regularly which resulted in the long duration of the programme.

Opportunities

1. If the literate and trained girls of the village are given the responsibility to teach the women in the absence of a teacher, programme could lead to greater success.
2. Some employment generation programmes could be supplemented with these programmes.
3. The technique of preparation of various food items and the technique of cultivation of vegetable can be used by the local people on a commercial basis to get additional income.
4. Awareness regarding health and hygiene that was surveyed through the participatory sessions, can help improve the physical and mental health of the community.
5. If taken in the right spirit, the message conveyed through the programmes might help to reduce the prevailing severe casticism in the society.

Limitations

1. The programmes that were introduced and carried out by the researcher in the study area were of limited durations and it is possible that what ever changes these programmes tried to bring about in the society might not be achieved to the full extent because of their discontinuity due to unavailability of any organisation or group to pursue them further.
2. The economic condition and the caste-wise stratification of the society prevented many willing women to join the programmes conducted by the researcher and get benefited out of them.

SUMMARY CONCLUSION AND SUGGESTION

Summary

The present study on the issue of 'empowerment of scheduled castes women' was conducted in the Naugarh Block of Chandauli district of Uttar Pradesh. This strip was selected purposively because of the following reasons :

(a) Its close proximity to Banaras Hindu University, which enabled the researcher to make frequent visits.

(b) The present of SCs community in majority in the study area.

(c) Well acquaintance with the local dialect of the people.

The target group included women of SC communities like Kharwar, Chero, Musahar, Harijans and Muslims.

The study was conducted through P.R.A. (Participatory Rural Appraisal) method which has an inbuilt mechanism to encourage participation of local people in the process of enquiry by -

Investigating local insights gained by interfacing with the common man, resulting in more effective 'research information' being located.

Involving local people in research and design of socio-economic endeavours so as to lead to increasing commitment and empowerment of local people.

It mainly focussed the socio-personal characteristics of women, their gender perception, the health, hygiene and sanitation condition and tried to evolve a possible solution to their various needs and problems.

This study has its own relevance as various other studies conducted earlier, were either based on the concept of data generation through conventional methods/surveys or were impact studies on women.

There was very little involvement of the actual beneficiaries in the policy formulation through such studies or surveys.

It is an established fact that women are poorly represented at the higher levels of decision-making process of the society. It is largely attributable to the prevailing cultural norms of gender behaviour and the perceived 'domestic' and 'reproductive, roles of women, which tends to adversely affect the education of girls. Negative attitudes towards sending girls to school, prejudice against retaining them in school, restrictions on 'mobility especially after puberty', early marriages, pressure to enter 'womenly courses' are known to effect the nature of participation of women in development process. These are reflections of the patriarchal values and attitudes which are dominant in the society.

Among poor families, the economic role of the girl child and her responsibilities in the households are obstacles to schooling.

The study area suffers from social and economic backwardness. This is mainly because of the fact that the area is basically a hilly region which is nearly two-third covered by forests. Also, the soil lacks fertility and is rocky in nature. The land size per family is marginal and because of this, agriculture as an occupation, fails to provide subsistence to the families. Since there are very limited job opportunities and the government sponsored employment generation programmes have failed to gain ground, local inhabitants mainly depend upon forest produce for their living. The major forest produce include Mahua, Tendu Patta and Piyar (Chiraungi). In Musahar village in particular, people are mainly engaged in pattal making activities which is also a forest produce. As can be well observed from the above discussion that the economic life of the area is rather harsh, the responsibility of earning rests mainly with the males but they are largely assisted by women folk. This, in turn, gives the males the right to take major decisions regarding family in particular and society in general.

The area also suffers from a rigid caste-wise stratification of the society, where in people belonging to one caste do not try to intermingle with those of other castes. The so-called 'high caste' people (Kharwar and Yadav) have generally been benefited, socially and economically, over the years.

It was observed that the low agricultural production and purchasing power ofthe people compelled them to virtually starve during few months (Ashwin - Kartik) of the year. Agriculture production is marked by high input-output ratio, thus making it an unprofitable occupation.

The socio-economic status is also reflected in the health and hygiene condition of the residents. People in the area suffer from various contagious diseases because of poor sanitation. No concrete effort has been made either by governmental or non-governmental organisations to improve the sanitation condition in the surveyed area. Similarly, the lack of proper medical facilities in the form of primary health centres, medical practitioners, immunisation programme etc. have contributed to a pathetic health condition of people especially women. Consequently, they are compelled to depend on 'local quacks' and untrained medical practitioners for their treatment.

Several intervention programmes were conducted in the study area during the period in which unconventional participatory sessions were held to guide the local women about a better hygienic life and it's importance and also about various new types of recipes and methods of food preservation. Unconventional literacy programmes of short duration were also held during period in which enthusiastic participation of interested women was observed. But, it should be generally agreed to that such programmes which are of very short duration can hardly benefit the target group until they are supplemented by several programmes of similar nature which are of longer duration and Circ in consonance with the desired objectives. These short duration programmes primarily aimed at generating awareness and building a rapport among rural folk. The role of Govt. agencies and NGOs can hardly be over emphasised in this regard.

CONCLUSION

The present study conducted through P.R.A. method in the Naugarh block of Chandauli district mainly focussed on the issue of women empowerment by identifying their problems/needs and evolving a possible solution to such problems. The participatory response was not very welcoming initially, but through repeated attempts by the researcher, the people slowly intermingled and relevant information could be gathered. The research experience gained throughout the study period shows how poverty and deprivation in poor households in remote areas of Naugarh block are reinforced due to gender position of women, which lends its impact both insidc and outside households. Since sustainable development at the micro level is best provided by poor women participating as major stake-holders in identifying their problems and designing suitable benefiting projects, the study mainly targeted this section of rural population. From the study the following conclusions have been arrived at:

(1) The social backwardness and gender discrimination are the main hindrances in the upliftment of women in the area.

(2) The male supremacy is evident in almost all spheres of life, be it the preference of child at birth or education or nutritional intake.

(3) Women fully realise that they are being discriminated against, but they lack will and courage to fight for their rights.

(4) Education of girl child is slowly picking up and this itself can act as a major catalyst in upgrading the status of women in the area.

(5) The area is devoid of proper schooling facilities. Although efforts have been made by several NGOs for providing basic and primary education, yet, the results are not very encouraging.

(6) As far as work-force participation is concerned, it has been found that women participation in agricultural activities, household activities

and in collecting forest produce is commendable, but still, the right to take major decisions rests with the males.

(7) The area is economically backward and there are very limited job opportunities available. The geographical location, soil type, irrigation facilities and land size are major contributors to low agricultural production with high input-output ratio. As such, they have to depend on forest produce for their subsistence.

(8) The availability of forest produce is not perennial in nature and hence certain period of the year are very critical when people have to survive with very little food.

(9) Life is very much dependent on forest for food and for such products which can earn them cash money. Fuel wood and wood for making shelter is also obtained from forest.

(10) Forest products like Mahua, Piyar (Chiraungi) and Tendu Patta are commercially viable, but the villagers have poor bargaining power as far as their selling price is concerned, because of lack of proper market and storage facilities. The products have to be sold as soon as they are collected.

(11) Excess exploitation of forest for fuelwood has resulted in large scale deforestation. The concept of forest conservation and afforestation is lacking among villagers.

(12) There is no provision of safeguarding crops and horticulture from wild animals. This, in turn, discourages women from taking up horticulture activities. Also, responsibility of women to guard their crops from being destroyed by such animals also increases manifold.

(13) The area lacks the availability of health and medical facilities. Government operated primary health centres and medical practitioners are rarely available in the area. Female medical practitioners are also rarely available which makes the treatment of women all the more difficult. Women hesitate to seek medical advise about their problems from male doctors because of their backwardness and social taboos. The immunisation programme for children is not very successful because of lack of such medical facilities.

(14) Poor nutritional intake and lack of proper hygiene result in frequent occurrence of contagious diseases among them.

(15) Lack of proper infrastructural facilities like roads, electricity supply, proper market for sale and purchase of goods, disposal of garbage and waste water, safe drinking water etc. hinders further development and progress in the area.

(16) Even though a number of NGOs are functional besides government agencies to provide the above mentioned facilities, inadequate coordination and cooperation and a tendency to supercede each other result in the non-fulfilment of the desired progress.

(17) The P.R.A. method which was successfully applied in the present study is found to be an effective technique for collecting and interpreting meaningful information from the actual beneficiaries. It emphasises the collaboration of actual beneficiaries in the interactive prioritisation, identification of problems, problem definition and alternative solutions. P.R.A. is regarded as a symbol of empowerment, participation, team building and vision creation. This method also helps in effective implementation of the proposed participatory intervention programmes.

(18) Various interventional programmes which were organised by the researcher prove quite beneficial and women of the study area enthusiastically participated in it and showed their willingness to learn and effectively use modern techniques of cooking and food preservation.

(19) Since the health and hygiene condition of the area is pathetic, proper training to improve the same was found very necessary. The researcher, through various interactive sessions tried to inculcate the importance of hygiene amongst the women folk. It was found that the message was clearly understood by them and they tried to change their habits towards a more hygienic and healthy life.

SUGGESTIONS

Keeping in view the above mentioned problems/needs of the area and conclusions derived thereupon, following viewpoints are being suggested for upliftment of the beneficiaries. Suggestion are broadly classified into:

(1) Health promotion.

(2) Education.

(3) Agriculture and forestry.

(4) Employment generation/wage earnings.

(5) Miscellaneous.

Health Promotion

Under health nutrition extension and health promotion of women, the following suggestions are listed:

(1) There should be a well equipped hospital and its sub-centres at the distance of not more than ten miles.

(2) Distribution of vitamin tablets and immunisation facilities to all the children, pregnant and lactating mothers should be done on a regular basis.

(3) Encouragement to adopt local ways of treating diseases should be promoted.

(4) Clean drinking water facilities should be provided in the villages where they are not available.

(5) Frequent visit/services of medical officers with lady staff should be provided to the patients suffering from serious illnesses in the area.

(6) Family planning measures should be provided to women on request.

(7) The inhabitants of area suffer from many communicable diseases. They should be educated about their precautions, causes and cures. For this, different audio-visual aids may be used.

(8) Hygiene and sanitation has a significant bearing upon the health of villagers, especially women. There should be privacy for bathing of women.

(9) Since a large number of unqualified practitioners are practising in the rural areas of Naugarh block, effort should be made to upgrade the skills and limit the scope of their practices so that exploitation by these practitioners can be discouraged.

(10) Revitalisation of local health traditions and local practitioners can play an important role throughout the area in health promotion.

(11) Voluntary sectors may play an effective role in imparting health education through schools and other forums.

(12) Linkages between early childhood care and primary education is essential. Efforts should be made to involve mothers and other adult women through home-based activities for development of women and children.

(13) People living in the tribal, hilly and arid regions have critical health status which is very much associated with problems of food security and other problems of underdevelopment. It is quite clear from the findings of study that there is a need to think about a subplan for the vulnerable and deprived regions. Major thrust must be to help them arrest the situation, through a well planned, adequately financed, community oriented Integrated Health and Development Programme with substantial participation of voluntary organisations. It is proposed that in these pockets, subsidised supply of basic staple food should be introduced, given the fact that our country has surplus food grain lying in stock and that a similar approach has given extremely good dividend in Andhra Pradesh and Tamil Nadu.

Education

Regarding facilitation of education, following can be suggested:-

(1) Taboos and unreasonable customs like not allowing women/girls to go out of their house for studies should be discouraged.

(2) There should be compulsory enrollment of rural girls in elementary schools by providing incentives to rural poor who are reluctant to send their children to schools.

(3) Maximum benefit from formal programmes would accrue when it is made more functional and given a more vocational basis.

(4) Women should be provided with a formal education so that they may themselves get benefited from modem science and technology in their life and do not become victims of their ignorance and backwardness.

(5) Development organisations can organise functional literacy classes for women during leisure hours. In these classes, some basic lessons for child care, health and nutrition, modem techniques of agriculture, can be given. The husband and wife duo should be approached, persuaded and educated by the organisations in the village to adopt family planning measures.

Suggestions regarding problem related to agriculture

(1) Introduction of new crop varieties that require less fertilisers and can cope with irregular rainfalls;

(2) Practice of improved crop rotation and inter-cropping;

(3) Timely control of pest;

(4) Use of natural and compost fertilisers;

(5) Application of soil conservation measures, irrigation in wet land drainage, residual moisture use, pond construction and irrigation;

(6) Encouragement of horticultural production;

(7) Changing cropping practices (Early Planting) ;

(8) Encouraging dry season irrigated vegetable crops;

(9) Encouragement of cash crops; and

(10) For fertility management, crop rotation and seed dressing can be done.

Suggestions for planning in forestry sector

(1) Pasture development so that animals have access to adequate fodder to meet their daily requirements.

(2) Plantation of species specifically useful for fuelwood purposes for convenience of women through their easy availability.

(3) Major thrust to be given on plantation in degraded forest area. Women groups from nearby villages can be formed and involved in this task.

(4) Ensuring people's participation in all these programmes especially small group participation whether facilitated by NGOs or the government.

(5) Emphasising soil conservation measures and plantation of such species which will be useful for conserving soil, again based on local priorities and needs.

(6) Fire protection to be ensured by forming small groups of people including women for management of forest.

(7) Plantation of medical plants/ herbs/ grasses for local use to be based on their priorities and needs as expressed through participatory methods.

(8) Plantation of spices on a commercial basis to gain long-term benefits.

A regular research centre for agriculture should be set up and Agricultural researchers should be encouraged to include women in all process of technology development, and linkages should be established between agricultural research institutes and women farmer associations to allow the flow of information relating to female oriented technologies.

The linkage between rural women and women professionals in the field of agriculture, veterinary science and allied areas can be strengthened through promotion of gender sensitive, location specific, inter-disciplinary research with compulsory involvement of rural women in planning technology, reassessment and evaluation.

Opportunities for wage employment

1. Cow dung products like cow-dung tooth powder, shampoo, NADEP compost etc. can be prepared for their own purpose and for sale too.

2. Organic farming through NADEP compost can enhance their production upto 20-30 per cent, which will add surplus to their consumption and sale.

3. Grading, packaging and sale of organic products and compost may earn them additional income.

4. Collection and sale of medicinal products from the forest.

5. Women can prepare jute bags, brooms, pickles, badi and papad for commercial purpose.

6. It seems that horticulture has a considerable scope in the area. Therefore, a comprehensive plan may be prepared for plantation of suitable varieties of fruits.

7. Spices may be grown in the area for commercial use. Tamarind has been experimented for the same and it can be grown on large scale to enhance the economic status of the people.

8. Development agencies will have to take a lead in introducing and strengthening household and village level industries based on local resources.

9. Palash flowers are found in abandoned quantity in the forest of study area. It may be collected and used for dyeing purposes and sale of which can contribute to their cash income.

10. Bee keeping or "Apiculture" has got a broader scope in these study villages. By assuming a stable occupation and source of income to rural women on an ongoing basis, it holds great promise to raise their standard of living, promote their economic independence and boost their socioeconomic status.

The job of apiculture is both interesting and instructive without making much demand on rural women's time for domestic chores or child care, energy and financial resources. The pursuit of apiculture does not require any sophisticated equipments. The technology employed is simple and within the grasp of even illiterate women. It is a non-land based and low investment activity, providing gainful employment and financial independence to rural women without moving away from their home.

11. Formation of seed bank

Women collect mahua, piyar, ber, amla etc. forest fruits and sell it at cheaper rate in the season. They can earn more profit if these products are stored and sold in off seasons.

Products	***Rate of Selling***	
	On Season	***Off Season***
Mahua	₹ 5.50/Kg	₹ 16.0/Kg
Piyar	₹ 40.0/Kg	₹ 60.0/Kg
Ber	₹ 4-5/Kg	₹ 10.0/Kg
Amla	₹ 6-8/Kg	₹ 12-14/Kg

12. There is a wide scope of making cane furnitures in the area as an abandon availability of forest weed i.e. called as Laltena. Little training in this regard can enhance their income with little or no expenditure of locally available raw materials.

13. Women can earn money from stitching the blouse, petticoat, baby frock, Kurta Paijama, Salwar Kurta etc. Resource required are stitching machine, training and market orientation.

Informational Network

In the age of information technology infrastructure facilities for rapid transactions of technologies up to the last person at the grass root level will have competitive advantage. There should be an apex body 'Central Information Organisation' to look after functioning of the system and information needs of the whole country. It will collect and collate information from various states regarding the research being done in various fields. 'State level Information Centre' may collect the information from centre system and coordinate at district level. It may also use the facilities of Radio and T.V. and other resources available to them to popularise new innovations. District Information Centre may take help of local media to give a message to every P.R.I. in that district. Village Information Centre, the last but most important link, may work in the information transfer in local dialect.

Rural women should be associated with developmental progammes right from planning stage to make the programme need based. A survey on the status of women, their problems, needs and expectations needs be conducted in each village. Based on the results of the survey, the need based projects to help solve the area specific problems must be formulated with active participation of rural women. Such needs may include discriminatory future roles, education, training, income generation, health etc. of girl and women depending upon their age. The unfelt needs are to be made felt needs through motivation for better results. Therefore, we need to highlight these motivational aspect to ensure better participation of rural women. Adequate opportunities, supportive institutions, proper education, vocational training and psychological support of male counterparts may help them to get empowered in real sense.

Effective commitments from government in terms of sizable investment and clean implementation are essential, given the dimension of the problems at hand. Serious efforts should be made either by government or NGOs in socio-economic areas of development like equal opportunity for education and development, equal status in family, equal wages for equal work, economic independence, suitable terms and conditions of work with due consideration to women's role in bearing and rearing the child and respect and dignity for women.

REFERENCES

References

1. Dwarakanath, H.D. (1999): DWCRA in Andhra Pradesh. Kurukshetra, Vol. 47, No. 12, pp. 14-18.
2. Government of India Census (Report 1991).
3. Narasimham, S. (1999) : Empowering Women. Sage Publication, New Delhi, pp. 22-34.
4. Rehana, K. (1998) : Safe Motherhood. Yojana, Vol. 42, No. 10, pp. 42-45.
5. Grover, I. (1993) : Effective Transfer of Household Technologies to Rural Women Clientele through Action Research and Experiential Learning Approach. Indian Journal of Adult Education, Vol. 54, No. 2, pp. 48-55.
6. Indian Economic Survey, (2000-2001) : Aklank Publications, p. 174.
7. Indian Economic Survey, (2001-2002) : p. 262.
8. Bhadauria, M. (1999) : Targeting Women for Development, Employment News, Vol. XXIV, No. 3, pp. 1-3.
9. Pattanaik, B.K. (1997) : Empowerment of Women and Rural Development. Yojana, Oct. 1997, pp. 24-27.
10. Bhadauria, M. (1999) : Targeting Women for Development. Employment News, Vol. XXIV, No. 3, pp. 1-3.
11 Country Report presented at the Fourth World Conference on Women, Beijing, 1995.
12. Devdas, R.P., Rajgopal, L.S. and Ramathilagan, A. (1988) : Horne Science Education and Women's Empowerment. Paper presented for Association of Women in Development Conference, Global Empowerment of Women, Washington.
13. Pillai, 1.K. (1989) : Women's March towards Equality. Yojana, Aug.
14. Global Conference (1988) : On Women Empowerment held in U.S.A.

15. Balliwala, Srilatha. (1994): The meaning of Women's Empowerment: The new concepts from Action in population, Policies Reconsidered Health, Empowerment and Rights, March, (1994), (Harvard Series on Population and International Health).
16. Apte, I.S. (1995) : Education and Women's Empowerment. Indian Journal of Adult Education, Vol. 56, No. 3, pp. 27-29.
17. Narasimham, S. (1999): Empowering Women. Sage Publication, New Delhi, pp. 22-34.
18. Prasad, C., Singh, R.P. and Krishnan, K.S., (1988) : Review of Research Studies on Women in Agriculture in India. Implications for Research and Extension, Indian Council of Agriculture Research.
19. Economic Survey of India, (2000-2001) and (2001-2002).
20. Ecoforum (1991) : Vol. 15, No. 2, July.
21. Rishi, P. (1997) : Women and Environment from Empowerment to Sustainable Development, Kurukshetra, (Jan.-Feb.) pp. 52-55.
22. Mukherji, N. (1995) : Participatory Rural Appraisal and Questionnaire Survey, Comparative Field Experience and Methodological Innovations, Concept Publishing, New Delhi.
23. Mukherji, N. (1993) : Participatory Rural Appraisal Methodology and Applications, Concept Publishing, New Delhi. p. 30.
24. Sarma, 1.S. and Mishra, A.S. (1998) : Participatory Rural Appraisal for Watershed Management, Published by Director, CSWCRT, Dehradun. p. 6.
25. Mukharji, A. (1995) : Participatory Rural Appraisal: Methods and applications in Rural Planning, Vikas Publishing House, New Delhi, p. 42.
26. Mukherji, N. (1993) : Participatory Rural Appraisal Methodology and Applications, Concept Publishing, New Delhi, p. 102.
27. Agony of life, Survey report from Naugarh, N.C.D.C. Varanasi.
28. Bendavid Val. Vol, A Vrom (1990) : Rural Area Development Planning A Review and Synthesis of Approaches. (Rome : FAO
29. Mukherji, A. (1993): Participatory Rural Appraisal Methodology and Applications, Concept Publishing, New Delhi, p. 67.
30. Bhadauria, M. (1999) : Targeting women for development, Employment News, Vol. XXIV, No. 23, pp. 1-2.
31. Shakuntala, Narsimham. (1999) : Empowering Women An Alternative Strategy from Rural India, Sage Publications, New Delhi.

32. Sachidananda, (1988) : Social change in village India, Concept Publishing House, Delhi.
33. Government of India, Eight Five Year Plan Document (preface), The Planning Commission, New Delhi.
34. Joseph, M. (1997) : Women Participation and Development Strategies. Kanishka Publishers and Distributors, New Delhi. p. 19.
35. Bhagya Lakashmi, J. (2000) : Women in Development. Employment News, Vol. XXV, No. 3, pp. 1-3.
36. Canadian International Development Agency, Coming of Age : CIDA and Women Development. Ministry of External Relations, Canada, 1987. p. 1.
37. Swaminathan, M.S. (1982) : The Role of Education and Research in Enhancing Rural Women's Incomc and Household Happiness. First J.P. Naik Memorial Lecture, New Delhi, September 11, 1982, Centre for Women's Development Studies.
38. Shirur, R. (1993) : Women Development Requires a Radical Approach. Indian Jr. of Adult Education, Vol. 54, No. 2, pp. 9-14.
39. Kashyap, S.K. and Gupta, S.P. (1998): Rural Development through poverty alleviation need for appropriate strategy, Kurukshetra, Vol. 46, No. 12, pp. 43-45.
40. Mukhwana, E.J. (2000) : 'Food Security and the Impact of Agricultural Development in Western Kenya : Problems and Opportunities. AgREN, Jan 2000, pp. 21-25.
41. Shakuntala, Narsimham. (1999): Empowering Women: An Alternative Strategy from Rural India, Sagc Publications, New Delhi, p. 236.
42. Boserup, E. (1970) : Women's Role in Economic Development, London, Allen and Unwin.
43. Duvvury, N. (1989) : Women in agriculture: A review of the Indian Literature. Economic and Political Weekly, Oct. 28, WS 96, WS 112.
44. Tiwari, P. (1999) : Involvement of females in Decision making process in Rural Sectors of parts of Thar Desert, Indian Journal of Adult Education, Vol. 60, No. 2, pp. 48-54.
45. Sardana, Gandhi, Hariya and Chamola (1988) : Role of women in agriculture: Farm women and Dairy cattle supplement one another. Journal of Extension system, Vol. 4, No. I, pp. 67-69.
46. Khanna, R. (1992) : Women in Panchmahals, in Book, Taking Charge: Women's health as empowerment, p. 3 SAHAJ Society for Health Alternatives, Gujarat.

47. Joshi, U. (1997) : Towards the Women Century. Social Welfare, pp. 29-32 (Oct. 1997).
48. British Parliamentary Papers. (1970) : 1881 and 1891 census, England and Wales. Irish University Press, Shannon Ireland, p. A3.
49. Ghosh, S. (2000) : Women in Agriculture; Employment News, Vol. XXV, No. 32, (4-10 Nov. 2000) pp. 1-2.
50. Oak, TJv1., *et al.,* Social and Institutional Framework of Female Participation in Agriculture. Indian Journal of Social Work, Oct., 1986, pp. 285-291.
51. Shobha, Volimieni. (1986) : Rural Women and Development - A study of Female Agricultural Labourers in Telangana, Indian Dissertation Abstracts, July-September, 1986, pp. 393-401.
52. Singh, Anil Kumar, Dutta, S.S. (1988) : Women and Development Promise and Realities, Centre for Women's Development Studies, New Delhi.
53. Agrawal, B. (1982) : Agricultural Mordernisation and Third World Women: Pointers from the Literature and an Empirical Analysis. Proceedings and Conclusions of the ILO Tripartite Asian Regional Seminar in India, April, 6-11, 1981, ILO, Genava, 1982.
54. Sinha, B.P., Verma, S.K. (1990) : Extension Education in Emancipation of Women in Agriculture. N.I.R.D., Course on Appropriate Technology for Rural Women, Hyderabad.
55. Chakravarty, S. (1990): Looking into Role and Participation of Women in Agricultural Production System and the Institutional Mechanism to Reach them - An analysis of the Experience in Coastal West Bengal, in NIRD, *ibid.*
56. Bhuyan, B., Tripathy, S.K. (1988): Role of Women in Agriculture: A study in Ganjam District of Odisha, Journal of Rural Development, Vol. 7(4), pp. 445-52.
57. Banu Fazila Lily, (1986) : The role of Rural Bangladesh: Women in Livestock Rearing in Leela Dube, *et al.,* (Ed) Visibility and Power Essays on Women in Society and Development, Oxford University Press, New Delhi.
58. Eswaran, S., Sekar, C. and Parvathi, S., (1998) : 'Women in Agriculture: A Case Study, Yojana, Dec. 1992, Vol. 42, No. 12, pp. 39-43.
59. Reddy, G.N. (1992) : An integrated Approach to Women's Development and Health Delivery Systems in Rural Areas. NIRD Experience, Journal of Rural Development, Vol. 11 (5), pp. 653-663.

60. Sen, K.R. (1989) : The nature of women's role in Economic Developmept in Mahajan V.S. (Ed) Women's Contribution to India's Economic and Social Development. Deep and Deep Publications, New Delhi.
61. Buxi, L.S. (1989) : Status of Women in India. Yojana, July 1- 15.
62. Sen, K.R. op.cit.
63. Duvvury, N. op.cit.
64. Chakravarty, S. op.cit.
65. Jyoti Pati, D. (2000) : Development Strategy Tribal participation and change: A study of Bondos. Yojana, Vol. 44, No. 4, April 2000, pp. 39-40.
66. Robert Chamber, (1997) : Whose reality counts? Putting the First Last, Intermediate Technology Publications, London, U.K. pp. XX+277, p. 122.
67. Adams, A., Roy D.A., *et al.,* (1993) : Participatory Methods to Assess Change in Health and Women's Lives BRAC-ICDDRB Joint Project in Matlab.
68. Bilgi, M. (1991) : Entering the Women's World: P.R.A. Experience with women in Village Nana Kandhasas, AKRSP.
69. Bilgi, M. (1992) : Entering Women's World: Through Men's Eyes: A Participatory Rural Appraisal at Boripitha, Netrang (AKRSP).
70. Francis, S., Devaram, J., *et al.* (1991) : Workshop on PRA for planning health projects, SPEECH.
71. Gujit, I. (1991): Women on Earth Gender Issues in Natural Resource Management, lIED.
72. Gujit, I. (1992) : Gender Differences and PRA, lIED.
73. Gujit, I. (1994) : Making a difference: Integrating gender analysis into P.R.A. Training, PRA Notes 19.
74. Haddad, L., Chung K., *et al.* (1993) : Alternative Approaches to Locating the Food and Nutritions Insecurity, International Food Policy Research Institute.
75. Jonfa, E. Haile Mariam Tabeje, *et al.,* (1991) : Participatory Modelling in North Umo, Ethopia, PRA Notes 14.
76. Krishnamurthy, R. (1994): Gender and Participatory Approaches: Implications and Experiences.
77. Sahu, M. and Tirkey, R, (1992) : A Little Experience conducted at Meclusbigang, PRA Notes 16.
78. Tolly, E., Benthey, M. (1994) : Participatory Methods for Research on Women's Reproductive Health, PRA Notes 16.

79. Vigoda, M. (1994) : Participatory Rural Appraisal in a Women's Health Education Project in Bangladesh, PRA Notes 14.

80. Wellbourn, A. (1991): PRA and the Analysis of Difference, PRA Notes 14.

81. Nevill, H.R. (1972): District Gazetteers of United Province, Vol. XXVI, Banaras.

82. Singh, K.K. and Maheshwari, J.K. (1985) : Forest in the life and economy of the tribals of Varanasi Districts, Uttar Pradesh. J. Econ. Tax. Bot. Vol. 6, No.1, pp. 109-116.

83. Agony of life, Survey report from Naugarh, N.C.D.C. Varanasi.

84. Mukharji, A. (1995) : Participatory Rural Appraisal: Methods and Applications in Rural Planning. Vikas Publishing House, New Delhi, p. 42.

85. Chambers, R. (1985) : Putting People First: Sociological Variables in Development Projects. John's Hopkins Press, Baltimore.

86. Mukharji, N. (1995) : Participatory Rural Appraisal: Methods and applications in Rural Planning. Vikas Publishing House, New Delhi, p. 30.

Appendices

Appendix - 1

नवगढ़ ब्लाक

1. जनसंख्या घनत्व (प्रति वर्ग किमी0)	:	214
2. अनु0जा0 व बनु0 जनजाति जनसंख्या प्रतिशत कुल जनसंख्या के आधार पर	:	42.2
3. चिकित्सालय एंव ग्रामीण स्वास्थ्य केन्द्र (प्रतिलाख जव)	:	6.6
4. बेसिक स्कूल संख्या	:	14
5. जिला मुख्यालय से विकास खण्ड की दूरी	:	92 किमी0
6. विकास खण्ड कार्यालय से निकटतम रेलवे स्टेशन की दूरी (मुगलसराय)	:	13 किमी0
7. कुल ग्राम	:	139
8. आबाद ग्राम	:	111
9. जनपद की ग्रामीण जनता की प्रति 10 वर्ष की जनसंख्या वृद्धि	:	45200 कुल
	:	23856 पु0
	:	21344 म0
10. गत दशक में वृद्धि	:	30.45
11. अनु0जाति/जनजाति की जनसंख्या	:	19082 कुल
	:	10012 पु0
	:	9070 म0
12. सारक्षर व्यक्ति	:	पु0 6778 (35.6 प्रतिशत)
	:	म0 1372 (8.2 प्रतिशत)
	:	कु0 8150 (22.8 प्रतिशत)

13. मान्यता प्राप्त शिक्षण : जू0बे0 स्कूल - 47

: सी0बे0 स्कूल - 7

: बालिक - नही

: हाई स्कूल - 2

संदर्भिका

सांख्यिकी पत्रिका

जनपद - वाराणसी, 1992

कार्यालय अर्थ एंव संख्या अधिकारी

राज्य नियोजन संस्थान

उ0प्र0

Local Folk Songs

Song-1

काहे करेला मोरे बाबूजी दोसंगी नातिया,
उही जन बाबा मेरे बेटवा जनमइला से,
उही जन बेटी जनमइला हमरे बाबू जी,
भैया के पढ़ावे के खातिर भेजिया स्कूलिया से
हमरे से घर पोतइला हमरे बाबू जी,
भैया के पढ़ावे के खातिर देसवा बिदेस भेजला
हमरे से बकरी चरइला हमरे बाबू जी,
भैया के खिलावे खातिर खोया मलाई दिहला,
हमरे के दल-भत मोहाला हमरे बाबू जी
भैया के पढ़ाई के नौकरी धाराई दिहला,
हमरे के स्कूल नही देयाइला हमरे बाबू जी
भैया के खबरिया खतिर जियरा तरस गइले
दूसरे से चिठिया बचइला हमरे बाबू जी
भैया के पढ़ावे खातिर रूपया पैसा दिहला
हमरे से बर्तन मजइला हमरे बाबू जी
माता हमरी बाली, हमके समझली हो
इक नजर तकली हो भैया बहिनी को
देसवा - बिदेसवा में भैया के नाम छपल
घरवा बैठ हम तो रोइली हमरे बाबू जी
नाहि देत गैया चाहे नाहि देत दहेजवा तू
पांच तक तो देखइला हमरे बाबम हमरे बाबम जी

List of Plants (Forest)

S.No.	*Common Name*	*Botanical Name*
1.	Sriphal	(Aegle marmelos corr)
2.	Koinadori	(Madhuca longifolia macb)
3.	Neem	(Azadirachta indica juss)
4.	Rendi	(Ricinus communis L.)
5.	Keonti	(Ventilago denticulata willd)
6.	Pilisarson	(Brassica compestris cass)
7.	Sakhu	(Shorea robusta goetn F.)
8.	Salai	(Boswellia serrata roxb)
9.	Karona	(Carissa opaca stpf)
10.	Silwaria	(Cassia fistula linn)
11.	Mujhani	(Celastrus paniculatus willd)
12.	Biskanara	(Crinum defixin)
13.	Tendu	(Diospyros exsculpta)
14.	Patharchatti	(Selaginella bryopteris bak)
15.	Karmhara	(Sterculia urens roxb)
16.	Dhera	(Alangium salvifo l ium wong)
17.	Amola	(Antidesma ghaesembilla gaertn)
18.	Satawar	(Asparagus racemosus willd)
19.	Barwat	(Basella alba linn)
20.	Piyar	(Buchanania lanzan spreng)
21.	Gainthi	(Dioscorea bulkifera linn)
22.	Khaniya	(D. pentaphylla linn;
23.	Mahua	(Madhuca indica)
24.	Kheksa	(Mamordica dioica roxb)
25.	Patalkohda	(Pueraria tuberosa DC)
26.	Khatjamun	(Syzygium heyneanum wall)
27.	Pidar	(Xeromphis uliginosa mahesh)
28.	Makoicha	(Ziziphus oenoplia mill)
29.	Sakhu	(Shorea robusta gaertn)
30.	Asna	(Terminalia alata heyne)

31.	Kadamb	(Adina cordifolia roxb)
32.	Shisham	(Dalbergia sissoo roxb)
33.	Gurchi	(Mitragyna parvifolia korth)
34.	Kumbi	(Careya Arborea roxb)
35.	Koraiya	(Holarrhena antidysenterica DC)
36.	Kus	(Desmostachya bipinnata linn)
37.	Jhoor	(Vetiveria zizanioids nash)
38.	Lukkhu	(Erogrostis gangetica steud)
39.	Khajuri	(Phoenix acaulis buch-ham)
40.	Banvar	(Ichnocarpus frutescens R. Br)
41.	Bajrahi	(Ixora arborca roxb)
42.	Meur	(Vitex negundo linn)
43.	Bans	(Dendrocalamus Strictus Nees)
44.	Asidh	(Lagerstra parviflora roxb)
45.	Kharhar	(Garturgida roxb)
46.	Katai	(Flacourtia indica merr)

NGOs Working in the Naugarh Block

NGOs	*Setup By and Head Office*	*Major Area of Development*
1. PEPUS Parayavaran Evam Prodaugiki Utthan Samiti	Hariram Kushwaha Jhusi, Allahabad	Handpump/well repairing (primary) Children education, water set management check dam, Farm bunding, Awareness generation among women gram pradhan regarding Panchyati Raj rules and regulations.
2. Gramya	Bindu Singh Banaras	(Primary) Children education, women organisation.
3. Devshila Banwasi Seva Prakalp	Suryakant Jalan	Primary Education.
4. Mahirshi Balmiki Seva Sansthan	Vishwa Hindu Parishad, Banaras	Children education primary to graduation level (Hostel facility at Naugarh Health).
5. Manav Seva Kendra	Jagat Narayan Singh Banaras	Primary education, Health and drinking water.
6. Adarsh Vidya Mandir	Vidya Bharti Organisation	Primary Education.
7. Nirbal Varga Utthan Samiti	Bachau Ram, Semara Kusahin, Naugarh	Awareness and motivation to child Education, immunisation.
8. Missionary Organisation	Christian Body	Health, Education.
9. N.C.D.C.	Y.K. Dubey Varanasi	Agriculture, Women Development Primary Education.

Index